BEYOND THE BIAS
AI'S ROLE IN FAIR HIRING &
EMPLOYER BRANDING

AF282466

Bibliografische Information der Deutschen Nationalbibliothek: Die Deutsche Nationalbibliothek verzeichnet diese Publikation in der Deutschen Nationalbibliografie; detaillierte bibliografische Daten sind im Internet über dnb.dnb.de abrufbar.

Verlag: BoD · Books on Demand GmbH, In de Tarpen 42, 22848 Norderstedt, bod@bod.de

Druck: Libri Plureos GmbH, Friedensallee 273, 22763 Hamburg

ISBN: 978-3-7693-8968-5

BEYOND THE BIAS

AI'S ROLE IN FAIR HIRING & EMPLOYER BRANDING

MIRANDA KINGSLEY

CONTENTS

INTRODUCTION

As we close the pages on this exploration of AI in hiring, the narrative emerges not just as a tale of technology, but as a crucial guide for reshaping the future of work. This book has illuminated the dual nature of AI: a tool of profound potential that, when wielded with care and insight, can dismantle the long-standing barriers of bias entrenched in hiring practices. Yet, it also serves as a reminder of the vigilance required to ensure that these tools do not perpetuate the very issues they aim to resolve.

The journey through these chapters has underscored the importance of a balanced approach. It is about harnessing technology to craft job descriptions that speak to a diverse audience, employing analytics to uncover hidden disparities in career advancement, and utilizing AI-driven insights to foster a culture of inclusivity. These steps are not mere enhancements to existing processes but are transformative shifts towards equity and fairness.

The narrative also stresses the necessity for transparency and ethical considerations in the deployment of AI. It calls for rigorous audits and continuous human oversight to safeguard against the replication of bias. As we look to the horizon, the potential for AI to drive real action in diversity and inclusion becomes apparent, moving beyond mere rhetoric to substantial, impactful change.

This book leaves us with a vision of a future where AI not only aids in fair hiring but also in cultivating workplaces that are truly representative and inclusive. It challenges leaders and practitioners to not only embrace these technologies but to lead with a commitment to fairness and equity. The path forward is clear: with thoughtful application and ethical stewardship, AI can indeed be a catalyst for a more equitable world of work.

Understanding Bias in AI

Defining Bias and Its Forms

Bias is a complex and multifaceted concept that significantly impacts decision-making processes, particularly in the realm of human resources and recruitment. At its core, bias refers to a systematic deviation from a standard of rationality or fairness. It manifests in various forms, each influencing perceptions and actions in distinct ways. Recognizing and understanding these forms is crucial for addressing bias effectively.

One prevalent form of bias is cognitive bias, which arises from the brain's attempt to simplify information processing. This type of bias can lead to errors in judgment and decision-making. Cognitive biases are numerous and include phenomena such as confirmation bias, where individuals favor information that confirms their preexisting beliefs, and anchoring bias, where they rely too heavily on the first piece of information encountered.

Another significant form of bias is implicit bias, which operates at a subconscious level. Implicit biases are the attitudes or stereotypes that affect our understanding, actions, and decisions unconsciously. These biases are often rooted in cultural stereotypes and can influence behavior in subtle but impactful ways. For instance, implicit gender bias may lead individuals to unconsciously associate certain roles or competencies with a specific gender, affecting hiring and promotion decisions.

Structural bias, meanwhile, is embedded in the systems and institutions that govern society. This form of bias results from policies and practices that systematically advantage or disadvantage certain groups. In the workplace, structural bias can manifest in various ways, such as unequal access to opportunities for advancement or disparities in pay. Addressing structural bias requires a comprehensive evaluation of organizational policies and the implementation of equitable practices.

A related concept is systemic bias, which refers to the broader societal patterns of discrimination and inequality. Systemic bias is perpetuated through historical and cultural norms and is often reflected in institutional practices. This form of bias necessitates a societal shift towards greater equality and inclusion, requiring concerted efforts from multiple stakeholders, including policymakers, organizations, and individuals.

Recognizing bias in all its forms is the first step towards mitigating its impact. In the context of AI-driven hiring and employer branding, it is essential to develop frameworks that identify and eliminate biases from algorithms and decision-making processes. AI offers powerful tools for analyzing language and patterns, but it also carries the risk of perpetuating existing biases if not carefully monitored and managed. Thus, a balanced approach that combines technological innovation with ethical oversight is necessary to ensure fairness and transparency.

By understanding the various forms of bias and their implications, organizations can work towards creating more equitable and inclusive environments. This involves not only addressing individual and institutional biases but also challenging the broader systemic patterns that sustain inequality. Through deliberate and informed action, it is possible to move beyond bias and foster a culture of fairness and diversity in all aspects of organizational life.

The Role of AI in Modern Hiring

Artificial intelligence (AI) has become a pivotal force in transforming modern hiring practices, introducing new efficiencies and challenges alike. As organizations strive to enhance their recruitment processes, AI offers innovative solutions that promise to streamline operations and reduce human error. However, the integration of AI in hiring is not without its complexities and necessitates a careful examination of its role in both improving and potentially complicating recruitment endeavors.

In recent years, AI has been increasingly employed to automate various stages of the hiring process, from candidate sourcing and resume screening to interview scheduling and even initial candidate assessments. By employing machine learning algorithms, companies can sift through vast quantities of applications swiftly, identifying candidates who best match the desired profiles. This not only accelerates the recruitment timeline but also allows human resources (HR) professionals to focus their energies on more strategic tasks, such as interviewing and candidate engagement.

Moreover, AI-driven tools are instrumental in reducing biases that traditionally plague recruitment processes. By analyzing language patterns and job descriptions, AI can help eliminate gendered language and other biases that might unconsciously deter diverse candidates from applying. This capability is critical in fostering a more inclusive workplace environment, as it ensures that job postings appeal to a broader audience, thereby enhancing diversity in candidate pools.

Despite these advantages, the deployment of AI in hiring is fraught with potential pitfalls. One significant concern is the inadvertent reinforcement of existing biases. If the data used to train AI systems is biased, the algorithms may perpetuate these biases, leading to unfair hiring practices. Therefore, it is crucial for organizations to implement robust checks and balances, ensuring that AI systems are audited regularly and that there is human oversight to rectify any biases that may arise.

Additionally, the transparency of AI processes remains a critical issue. Candidates may feel uneasy about being evaluated by an algorithm, particularly if the criteria used are not fully disclosed. To address these concerns, companies must prioritize transparency and communication, clearly explaining how AI tools are used in the hiring process and the measures taken to ensure fairness and objectivity.

Furthermore, the ethical implications of AI in hiring cannot be overlooked. The use of AI raises questions about data privacy and consent, necessitating stringent data protection measures to safeguard candidate information. Organizations must navigate these ethical considerations carefully, balancing the benefits of AI with the ethical duty to protect individual rights.

Ultimately, the role of AI in modern hiring is both transformative and complex. As organizations continue to integrate AI into their recruitment strategies, they must do so with a commitment to ethical practices, transparency, and continuous improvement. By harnessing the full potential of AI while addressing its challenges, companies can create more efficient, fair, and inclusive hiring processes that benefit both employers and job seekers alike.

Historical Context of Bias in Technology

The evolution of technology has always been intertwined with the social dynamics of its time, reflecting both the progress and the prejudices of the societies that birthed it. As we delve into the historical context of bias in technology, it becomes evident that technological advancements have often mirrored societal biases, from the earliest tools to the sophisticated algorithms of today. This reflection is not merely coincidental but is rooted in the very fabric of technological development, influenced by the cultural and ethical norms of each era.

In the early days of computing, the field was predominantly male-dominated, a trend that was a direct consequence of societal norms that limited women's roles in science and technology. This gender bias was not just a reflection of the workforce composition but also influenced the design and application of early technologies. For instance, the development of software and hardware often ignored the needs and perspectives of women, leading to a technological landscape that was skewed towards male users.

This bias was further perpetuated by the education systems and hiring practices of the time, which discouraged women from pursuing careers in technology.

As technology progressed, so did the complexity of the biases embedded within it. The advent of the internet and digital communication tools in the late 20th century brought about new forms of bias, particularly in the representation and visibility of marginalized groups. The algorithms that powered search engines and social media platforms were often trained on datasets that lacked diversity, leading to outcomes that favored dominant cultural narratives while marginalizing others. This digital bias was not merely a technical oversight but a reflection of the broader societal inequalities that existed offline.

In recent years, the rise of artificial intelligence and machine learning has brought the issue of bias in technology to the forefront. AI systems, which are often perceived as objective and impartial, are in fact deeply influenced by the data on which they are trained. This data, collected from a world rife with inequalities, inevitably carries the biases of its origin. As a result, AI systems can perpetuate and even amplify existing biases, from racial profiling in law enforcement to gender discrimination in hiring processes.

Understanding the historical context of bias in technology is crucial for developing more equitable and inclusive technological solutions. It requires a critical examination of how past biases have shaped current technologies and a commitment to addressing these issues at their root. This involves not only diversifying the workforce involved in technological development but also rethinking the ethical frameworks that guide this development.

Moreover, as technology continues to evolve, it is imperative to remain vigilant about the new forms of bias that may emerge. This involves continuous monitoring and auditing of technological systems to ensure they serve all segments of society fairly. By learning from the past, we can work towards a future where technology truly acts as an equalizer, rather than a perpetuator of existing disparities.

Case Studies of Bias in AI Systems

Artificial intelligence systems have become integral to various sectors, offering unprecedented efficiency and insights. However, these systems can also perpetuate and even exacerbate existing biases if not carefully designed and implemented. Through examining case studies, we can better understand how biases manifest in AI systems and what measures can be taken to mitigate these issues.

One prominent example of bias in AI systems is found in facial recognition technology. These systems have been widely adopted in security and law enforcement, yet numerous studies have shown that they often have higher error rates when identifying individuals from minority ethnic groups. This discrepancy arises from the datasets used to train these models, which are frequently skewed towards certain demographics, leading to a lack of representation. As a result, individuals from underrepresented groups are more likely to be misidentified, which can have serious consequences, including wrongful arrests. Efforts to address these biases have included diversifying training datasets and implementing rigorous testing protocols to ensure fair performance across different demographic groups.

In the realm of recruitment, AI systems are increasingly used to screen resumes and identify potential candidates. However, these systems can inadvertently reinforce gender and racial biases present in historical hiring data. For instance, if a company historically hired more men for engineering roles, an AI system trained on this data might favor male candidates. To counteract this, companies have started to adopt strategies such as anonymizing resumes and using AI to identify and remove biased language from job descriptions, thus promoting a more inclusive hiring process.

Another significant case involves AI-driven credit scoring systems, which are used to determine the creditworthiness of individuals. These systems can perpetuate socioeconomic biases if they rely heavily on data points like zip codes, which correlate with economic status and racial demographics. This can result in unfair credit assessments for individuals from marginalized communities. To mitigate such biases, financial institutions are exploring the use of alternative data sources and developing algorithms that prioritize fairness and transparency.

Healthcare is another sector where AI bias has been critically examined. Predictive models used to allocate medical resources or assess patient risks can exhibit biases if they are trained on non-representative data. For example, a model predicting patient outcomes might perform poorly on minority groups if the training data lacks diversity. Addressing this requires a concerted effort to ensure data used in healthcare AI reflects the diversity of the patient population and is regularly audited for bias.

These case studies highlight the pervasive issue of bias in AI systems and underscore the importance of proactive measures to address them. As AI continues to evolve, it is crucial for developers, policymakers, and stakeholders to collaborate on creating systems that are not only effective but also equitable and just. By learning from past mistakes and implementing robust ethical guidelines, we can harness the power of AI to benefit all members of society.

The Need for Ethical AI in HR

In the rapidly evolving landscape of Human Resources, Artificial Intelligence (AI) has emerged as a pivotal tool, promising to revolutionize the way organizations manage their workforce. However, as AI systems become more integrated into HR processes, it is crucial to address the ethical implications associated with their use.

The integration of AI in HR is not just about leveraging technology for efficiency but also about ensuring that these systems operate within an ethical framework that upholds fairness and transparency.

AI systems, by their very design, process vast amounts of data to identify patterns and make decisions. In HR, these capabilities are harnessed to streamline recruitment processes, evaluate employee performance, and even predict future workforce trends. However, this reliance on data-driven decision-making introduces the risk of perpetuating existing biases if not carefully managed. AI systems learn from historical data, and if this data reflects social prejudices or discriminatory practices, the AI can inadvertently reinforce these biases.

The ethical use of AI in HR requires a concerted effort to identify and mitigate these biases. This involves not only auditing the data used to train AI systems but also implementing checks and balances to ensure that AI-driven decisions are fair and equitable. Transparency is key in this context. Organizations must be open about how AI systems are used in HR processes and the criteria they use to make decisions.

This transparency builds trust among employees and candidates, who need assurance that AI will not be a tool for discrimination.

Moreover, ethical AI in HR goes beyond just addressing biases; it encompasses the broader responsibility of ensuring that AI systems respect the privacy and autonomy of individuals. With AI's ability to analyze personal data at an unprecedented scale, there is a pressing need for robust data protection measures. Organizations must establish clear guidelines on data usage and ensure compliance with legal and ethical standards to protect individual privacy.

Human oversight is another critical component of ethical AI in HR. While AI can provide valuable insights and recommendations, the final decision-making should rest with humans. This ensures that decisions are contextualized within human values and ethical considerations, something AI systems are not yet capable of fully understanding or implementing.

The ethical deployment of AI in HR also involves ongoing evaluation and adaptation. As AI technology evolves, so too should the frameworks governing its use. Continuous monitoring and feedback mechanisms are essential to identify any unintended consequences of AI implementation and to make necessary adjustments. This proactive approach enables organizations to harness the benefits of AI while minimizing potential harms.

In conclusion, the need for ethical AI in HR is paramount to ensure that technological advancements do not come at the cost of fairness and equity. By prioritizing transparency, fairness, and human oversight, organizations can create an ethical framework that not only enhances HR processes but also fosters a more inclusive and equitable workplace. This commitment to ethical AI will ultimately drive sustainable success and innovation in the HR domain.

AI-Powered Language Analysis

Identifying Biased Wording

In the realm of human resources and recruitment, language plays a pivotal role in shaping perceptions and influencing decisions. Language, however, can be a double-edged sword. While it can be used to create inclusive environments, it can also perpetuate biases and stereotypes if not carefully managed. This chapter delves into the critical task of identifying biased wording in job postings and employer branding materials, a necessary step towards fostering diversity and inclusion in the workplace.

Biased wording often manifests subtly, embedded in job descriptions and organizational communications. These biases can deter qualified candidates from diverse backgrounds, ultimately affecting the diversity of the talent pool. For instance, words that emphasize aggressiveness or competitiveness might discourage women or individuals from cultures that value collaboration over competition. Similarly, terms that suggest a preference for younger candidates can alienate experienced professionals who might otherwise bring valuable insights to a role.

The advent of artificial intelligence (AI) offers powerful tools to address these challenges. AI algorithms can analyze language patterns in job postings to identify words or phrases that may carry unintended biases. By leveraging natural language processing techniques, AI can flag potentially problematic language, allowing recruiters to revise and refine their postings to be more inclusive. This not only broadens the appeal of job advertisements but also aligns with ethical hiring practices that promote fairness.

Furthermore, AI-driven language analysis can be instrumental in crafting employer branding messages that resonate with a diverse audience. Employer branding is crucial for attracting a wide range of talent, and inclusive language is a key component. Through AI, organizations can ensure that their branding efforts do not inadvertently exclude any demographic groups. This involves not just the removal of biased language but also the proactive inclusion of language that reflects the company's commitment to diversity and equity.

Beyond just identifying biased wording, there is a need for a comprehensive approach to eliminate these biases from the recruitment process. This includes training HR professionals and recruiters to recognize and avoid biased language and fostering a culture of awareness and sensitivity. Regular audits of job postings and recruitment materials can ensure ongoing compliance with inclusive language standards.

Moreover, organizations must be vigilant about the potential for AI itself to introduce or perpetuate biases. AI systems are only as unbiased as the data they are trained on, and without careful oversight, they can reinforce existing stereotypes. Therefore, it is essential to implement transparent AI auditing processes and maintain human oversight to ensure that AI tools contribute positively to diversity and inclusion efforts.

In sum, identifying biased wording is a foundational step in creating an equitable recruitment process. By utilizing AI technologies and cultivating an inclusive mindset, organizations can overcome linguistic barriers to diversity, thereby enriching their talent pool and enhancing their organizational culture.

This proactive approach not only meets the ethical imperatives of modern business but also positions companies to thrive in an increasingly diverse and dynamic world.

Creating Inclusive Job Descriptions

Crafting job descriptions that invite a diverse range of applicants is a critical step toward fostering an inclusive workplace. The language and structure of job postings significantly influence the types of candidates attracted to a position. By focusing on inclusivity from the outset, organizations can begin to dismantle systemic biases that often pervade traditional hiring practices.

One of the fundamental aspects of creating inclusive job descriptions is the careful selection of language. Words carry inherent biases that can inadvertently discourage certain groups from applying. For instance, terms traditionally associated with gender roles or aggressive business vernacular may deter female candidates or those from different cultural backgrounds.

To counteract this, job descriptions should be crafted with gender-neutral language and a focus on universal competencies rather than culturally specific attributes.

Moreover, emphasizing the essential skills and experiences required for a position, rather than a long list of preferred qualifications, can broaden the pool of potential applicants. This approach not only reduces the barriers for those who may possess the necessary skills but lack formal credentials but also encourages applications from diverse backgrounds. By highlighting core competencies and demonstrating a commitment to training and development, organizations signal their openness to candidates who bring varied experiences and perspectives.

Another strategy involves scrutinizing the tone and style of job descriptions. A collaborative and welcoming tone can make a position more appealing to a wider audience. Employers should avoid jargon and industry-specific language that may not be universally understood. Instead, descriptions should be clear, concise, and focused on what the candidate can expect in terms of responsibilities and opportunities for growth.

Furthermore, transparency in job postings about the company's commitment to diversity and inclusion can attract candidates who value these principles. Explicitly stating the organization's DEI (Diversity, Equity, and Inclusion) goals and the specific steps it is taking to achieve them can reassure prospective employees that diversity is not merely a buzzword but a genuine priority.

Incorporating feedback from current employees who represent diverse groups can also enhance the inclusivity of job descriptions. These individuals can provide insights into how language and presentation might be perceived by potential candidates from underrepresented backgrounds. Consequently, involving such stakeholders in the drafting process can help identify and eliminate subtle biases that might otherwise be overlooked.

Finally, leveraging technology, such as AI-driven language analysis tools, can assist in identifying biased language and suggesting more inclusive alternatives. These tools can analyze job descriptions for patterns that may inadvertently favor certain demographics, enabling recruiters to make data-informed adjustments.

Through these concerted efforts, creating inclusive job descriptions becomes more than a procedural task; it transforms into a strategic initiative aimed at building a workforce that reflects diverse perspectives and talents. By setting the right tone and expectations from the beginning, organizations pave the way for a more equitable and inclusive hiring process.

AI Tools for Language Analysis

In the realm of artificial intelligence, tools for language analysis have emerged as transformative assets, particularly in the context of human resources and employer branding. These tools leverage the power of AI to dissect and interpret linguistic patterns, offering insights that can significantly enhance the inclusivity and effectiveness of communication within organizations. AI-driven language analysis is pivotal in identifying and eliminating biases that may be inadvertently embedded in job postings and recruitment materials. By analyzing the language used, AI can highlight potentially discriminatory terms or phrases that could deter diverse candidates from applying. This capability allows organizations to craft job descriptions that are more inclusive and appealing to a broader talent pool.

Moreover, AI tools can be employed to evaluate and refine employer branding messages, ensuring they resonate with a diverse audience. By analyzing linguistic nuances, these tools help in crafting messages that are not only inclusive but also reflective of the organization's commitment to diversity, equity, and inclusion (DEI). This approach not only attracts a wider range of candidates but also strengthens the organization's brand as a leader in DEI initiatives.

Beyond recruitment, AI language analysis plays a crucial role in assessing and transforming workplace culture. Sentiment analysis, a subset of language analysis, can be used to gauge employee perceptions and attitudes towards DEI efforts. By analyzing internal communications and feedback, AI can uncover underlying sentiments and resistance to change. This information is invaluable for tailoring DEI initiatives and training programs to address specific cultural barriers and foster a more inclusive environment.

Furthermore, AI tools for language analysis are instrumental in facilitating anonymous employee feedback and DEI reporting. By ensuring anonymity, these tools encourage honest feedback from employees, which can be analyzed to identify areas for improvement.

This feedback loop is essential for continuous improvement and accountability in DEI efforts.

The implementation of AI in language analysis also necessitates a strong ethical framework. As with any AI application, there is a risk of reinforcing existing biases if these tools are not used judiciously. It is imperative to ensure that AI systems are designed and audited to be fair, transparent, and unbiased. This requires ongoing monitoring and human oversight to validate the outputs of AI tools and ensure they align with ethical standards and organizational goals.

In conclusion, AI tools for language analysis offer significant potential to transform how organizations approach diversity and inclusion. By providing insights into linguistic patterns and sentiments, these tools enable organizations to create more inclusive and appealing communications, foster a culture of openness and accountability, and ultimately drive meaningful change in workplace dynamics. However, the successful integration of these tools requires a commitment to ethical practices and continuous evaluation to ensure they contribute positively to the organization's DEI objectives.

Challenges in Language Neutrality

In the realm of artificial intelligence and automated systems, the pursuit of language neutrality presents a unique set of challenges. Language neutrality refers to the ability of AI systems to operate without favoring any particular language, dialect, or cultural nuance, ensuring fair and unbiased communication across diverse linguistic backgrounds. However, achieving true language neutrality is fraught with complexities that stem from both technical and cultural dimensions.

One of the primary challenges in attaining language neutrality is the inherent bias present in training data. AI systems are trained on vast amounts of text data, which often reflect the biases and stereotypes of the societies from which they originate. This can result in AI models that inadvertently perpetuate existing linguistic biases, favoring dominant languages or dialects over less prevalent ones. Consequently, there is a significant risk of marginalizing languages that are less represented in data sets, leading to unequal treatment in AI-driven interactions.

Moreover, the nuances of language, such as idioms, slang, and cultural references, pose a significant hurdle to language neutrality. These linguistic elements are deeply embedded in cultural contexts and can vary widely even within the same language. AI systems must navigate these subtleties to provide accurate and equitable responses. However, the complexity of understanding and correctly interpreting these nuances often leads to errors or misinterpretations, particularly in languages or dialects that are underrepresented in AI training data.

Another challenge arises from the technical limitations of natural language processing (NLP) technologies. While advancements have been made, current NLP models often struggle with less commonly used languages, which may lack the extensive corpora available for more dominant languages. This disparity in resource availability can lead to performance gaps, where AI systems are less effective in processing and generating text in minority languages. Addressing this issue requires significant investment in developing linguistic resources and improving NLP techniques for a wider range of languages.

Furthermore, the continuous evolution of language adds another layer of complexity. Languages are dynamic, constantly evolving with new words, expressions, and usages. AI systems must be capable of adapting to these changes to maintain language neutrality. This necessitates ongoing updates and refinements to AI models, which can be resource-intensive and challenging to implement consistently across all languages.

Efforts to overcome these challenges involve both technical and ethical considerations. From a technical standpoint, developing more inclusive and diverse training datasets is crucial. This includes actively seeking out and incorporating data from a wide array of languages and dialects, as well as continuously monitoring and mitigating biases in AI outputs. Ethically, there is a need for frameworks that prioritize language equity, ensuring that AI systems do not disadvantage speakers of minority languages.

In summary, achieving language neutrality in AI systems is a multifaceted challenge that requires a concerted effort to address both technical limitations and cultural biases.

By fostering greater inclusivity in AI development and actively working to eliminate linguistic biases, we can move towards a more equitable digital landscape that respects and values linguistic diversity.

Future Trends in Language AI

As we look ahead, the evolution of language AI is set to transform numerous facets of our lives, particularly in how we interact with technology and each other. One prominent trend is the increasing sophistication of natural language processing (NLP) models, which are becoming more adept at understanding context, nuance, and even emotional tone. This advancement is poised to enhance user experiences across various platforms, from customer service chatbots to virtual assistants, making interactions more intuitive and human-like.

Moreover, the integration of AI in language translation is breaking down linguistic barriers at an unprecedented rate. With continual improvements in accuracy and fluency, AI-driven translation tools are facilitating smoother global communication, fostering cross-cultural collaborations, and expanding access to information. This trend is particularly significant in educational and professional settings, where language can often be a barrier to entry.

Another area of rapid development is AI's role in content creation. Language AI is increasingly being utilized to generate articles, reports, and even creative writing, offering tools that assist rather than replace human creativity. This capability is transforming industries such as journalism, marketing, and entertainment, where the demand for content is ever-growing. By automating routine writing tasks, AI is enabling professionals to focus on higher-level strategizing and creative endeavors.

In the realm of accessibility, language AI is making strides in supporting individuals with disabilities. Speech recognition and synthesis technologies are improving communication for those with hearing or speech impairments, while text-to-speech and speech-to-text tools are becoming more accurate and user-friendly. These advancements are crucial in creating more inclusive environments, both online and offline.

Privacy and ethical considerations continue to be at the forefront of AI development. As language models grow more powerful, the need for robust ethical frameworks becomes imperative to ensure that these technologies are used responsibly and do not perpetuate biases or violate privacy. The development of transparent AI systems, coupled with regulatory oversight, is essential to maintain public trust and ensure equitable outcomes.

Finally, the future of language AI is likely to be characterized by greater personalization. AI systems are increasingly capable of tailoring interactions based on individual preferences and behaviors, offering more customized and relevant experiences. This trend is evident in personalized marketing, adaptive learning platforms, and personalized news feeds, where AI helps filter and present information in ways that align with user interests and needs.

Overall, the future of language AI holds immense promise, with the potential to revolutionize communication, accessibility, and personalization. As these technologies continue to evolve, they will undoubtedly play a pivotal role in shaping the digital landscape, offering new opportunities and challenges alike.

It is essential for stakeholders to navigate these changes thoughtfully, ensuring that the benefits of language AI are realized while addressing the ethical and societal implications that accompany its progression.

Inclusive Employer Branding

Defining Employer Branding

Employer branding is a strategic approach that involves shaping the perception of a company as an employer of choice. It is a multifaceted concept that extends beyond mere recruitment tactics, embedding itself into the core of a company's identity and values. At its heart, employer branding is about creating a compelling narrative that resonates with potential and current employees, aligning their personal values with the organizational mission and culture.

The concept of employer branding is rooted in marketing principles, adapted to focus on the employment experience rather than consumer products. It involves a deliberate effort to communicate an organization's values, culture, and work environment in a manner that attracts and retains talent.

This involves not only the creation of attractive job postings but also the cultivation of a positive work culture that is reflected in every interaction an employee has with the organization.

Employer branding is increasingly seen as a crucial component of a company's overall brand strategy. In today's competitive job market, where talent is often scarce, having a strong employer brand can be a significant differentiator. Companies with robust employer brands are more likely to attract top talent, reduce hiring costs, and improve employee retention. This is because potential employees are more inclined to apply to organizations that they perceive to be desirable places to work.

A well-defined employer brand is built on authenticity and transparency. It requires a clear understanding of what makes the organization unique and how it can offer a fulfilling career path to its employees. This means not only communicating the benefits and perks of working at the company but also highlighting the potential challenges and opportunities for growth. By setting realistic expectations, companies can attract candidates who are genuinely interested in the organization's mission and are more likely to thrive in its environment.

The process of defining an employer brand involves several key steps. First, it requires an internal assessment to identify the organization's strengths and weaknesses as an employer. This involves gathering feedback from current employees, analyzing employee turnover rates, and understanding the company culture. Next, it involves crafting a value proposition that clearly articulates the benefits of working for the organization. This proposition should be communicated consistently across all platforms, from job postings to social media channels.

Moreover, employer branding is not a one-time effort but an ongoing process that involves continuous engagement with employees. It requires regular updates to the employer value proposition to reflect changes within the organization and the broader market. Companies must also be prepared to adapt their strategies in response to feedback from employees and candidates.

Ultimately, employer branding is about building a relationship between the employer and employee that is based on mutual respect and shared goals. It is about creating an environment where employees feel valued and motivated to contribute to the company's success.

By investing in employer branding, organizations can create a sustainable competitive advantage that attracts and retains the best talent, driving long-term success.

Strategies for Inclusive Branding

In an era where diversity and inclusion are more than just buzzwords, businesses are increasingly recognizing the importance of creating brands that resonate with a broader audience. Inclusive branding is not only about reaching a wider demographic but also about building a brand that reflects the values of equity, diversity, and inclusion. This approach requires a strategic alignment of brand messaging, visual identity, and customer interaction that speaks to the diverse backgrounds and experiences of potential customers.

The first step in developing an inclusive brand is to understand the diverse needs and expectations of different customer segments. This involves conducting thorough market research to identify the unique characteristics and preferences of various demographic groups. By gaining insights into cultural nuances, language preferences, and social values, brands can tailor their messaging to resonate with a diverse audience. This research-driven approach helps in crafting messages that are not only inclusive but also authentic and relatable.

Another critical strategy is to ensure representation in all forms of brand communication. This means featuring diverse individuals in advertising campaigns, using inclusive language in marketing materials, and ensuring that the brand's voice reflects the diversity of its audience. Representation matters because it helps customers see themselves in the brand, fostering a sense of belonging and connection. Brands should strive to move beyond tokenism by genuinely engaging with diverse communities and reflecting their stories and experiences in brand narratives.

Inclusivity should also extend to the design and functionality of products and services. Brands need to consider accessibility in product design, ensuring that their offerings are usable by people with different abilities. This can involve anything from creating packaging that is easy to open for individuals with physical disabilities to designing websites that are accessible to people with visual impairments.

By prioritizing accessibility, brands demonstrate their commitment to inclusivity and expand their reach to underserved markets.

Furthermore, brands must engage in ongoing dialogue with diverse communities to build trust and credibility. This can be achieved through partnerships with organizations that advocate for underrepresented groups, participating in community events, and seeking feedback from diverse customer segments. By actively involving these communities in the brand's evolution, businesses can ensure that their branding strategies remain relevant and respectful.

Finally, it is crucial for brands to measure the impact of their inclusive branding efforts. This involves setting clear objectives, collecting data on customer demographics and engagement, and analyzing this data to assess the effectiveness of branding strategies. By continuously evaluating and refining their approach, brands can make informed decisions that drive inclusion and foster long-term customer loyalty.

Inclusive branding is not a one-time initiative but an ongoing commitment to embracing diversity in all aspects of a business. By adopting these strategies, brands can not only enhance their market position but also contribute to a more equitable and inclusive society. The journey towards inclusive branding requires dedication and intentionality, but the rewards in terms of customer loyalty and brand reputation are well worth the effort.

AI's Role in Branding

Artificial intelligence (AI) is transforming the landscape of branding by offering innovative tools and methods to enhance brand recognition and loyalty. One of the primary ways AI contributes to branding is through advanced data analytics. By analyzing vast amounts of consumer data, AI can identify patterns and trends that human analysts might overlook. This capability allows brands to tailor their marketing strategies to meet the specific needs and preferences of their target audience, thereby fostering a more personalized and engaging customer experience.

AI also plays a crucial role in enhancing customer interactions. Chatbots and virtual assistants, powered by AI, provide instant and efficient customer service, ensuring that consumers receive timely responses to their inquiries. This not only improves customer satisfaction but also frees up human resources to focus on more complex tasks. Furthermore, AI-driven sentiment analysis helps brands gauge public perception by analyzing social media interactions and online reviews. This insight enables companies to adjust their branding strategies proactively, addressing potential issues before they escalate.

In addition to improving customer interactions, AI aids in content creation and optimization. AI algorithms can generate content ideas based on trending topics and consumer interests, ensuring that the brand's messaging remains relevant and engaging. Moreover, AI tools can optimize content for search engines, enhancing visibility and reach. This is particularly important in the digital age, where brands compete for attention in a crowded online marketplace.

AI's role in branding extends to visual identity as well. Through machine learning algorithms, AI can analyze design trends and consumer preferences to suggest improvements to a brand's visual elements, such as logos and color schemes. This ensures that the brand's visual identity remains modern and appealing to its audience.

However, the integration of AI in branding is not without challenges. One significant concern is the ethical use of AI, particularly regarding data privacy. Brands must ensure that they use consumer data responsibly and transparently, adhering to privacy regulations and maintaining consumer trust. Additionally, there is a risk of over-reliance on AI, which can lead to a loss of the human touch in branding. It is crucial for brands to strike a balance between leveraging AI's capabilities and maintaining authentic human connections with their audience.

Despite these challenges, the potential of AI in branding is immense. By harnessing AI's analytical and creative capabilities, brands can create more personalized, efficient, and impactful branding strategies. As AI technology continues to evolve, it will undoubtedly open new avenues for brands to connect with their audiences and strengthen their market position. In this rapidly changing digital landscape, embracing AI's role in branding is not just an option but a necessity for brands aiming to thrive in the competitive market.

Assessing Branding Impact

In the modern business landscape, branding has evolved beyond conventional marketing strategies and now plays a pivotal role in shaping organizational identity, especially in the context of employer branding. The effectiveness of these branding efforts is crucial not only for attracting potential employees but also for retaining current staff and ensuring alignment with organizational values. Assessing the impact of branding initiatives involves a comprehensive evaluation of how these efforts influence perceptions both internally and externally.

A critical aspect of assessing branding impact is understanding the perception of the brand among the target audience. This involves gathering data on how the brand is viewed by potential candidates, current employees, and even competitors. Surveys, interviews, and social media analytics can provide valuable insights into brand perception. These tools help in identifying the strengths and weaknesses of the current branding strategy, allowing organizations to refine their approaches to better meet the expectations of their audience.

Furthermore, the alignment of branding with organizational values and culture is essential. A brand that authentically represents its core values is more likely to attract individuals whose personal values align with those of the organization. This congruence not only enhances employee satisfaction and engagement but also reduces turnover rates. Thus, assessing branding impact should include an evaluation of how well the brand communicates its values and whether these values are reflected in the workplace culture.

The role of technology, particularly AI, in assessing branding impact cannot be overstated. AI tools can analyze large volumes of data to identify trends and patterns in how the brand is perceived. For instance, sentiment analysis can be employed to gauge public perception of the brand across various platforms. Additionally, AI-driven analytics can provide insights into the effectiveness of branding campaigns by tracking engagement metrics and conversion rates.

Another important factor in assessing branding impact is measuring the return on investment (ROI) of branding initiatives. This involves analyzing the financial and non-financial benefits derived from branding efforts. Financial metrics might include increased revenue, market share, and cost savings from reduced recruitment expenses. Non-financial metrics could encompass enhanced brand recognition, improved employee morale, and a stronger organizational reputation.

Moreover, the impact of branding should be assessed in the context of diversity, equity, and inclusion (DEI). A strong employer brand should reflect a commitment to DEI, as this is increasingly important to both current and prospective employees. Evaluating the extent to which branding efforts promote a diverse and inclusive workplace can provide insights into the brand's effectiveness in appealing to a broad audience.

In conclusion, assessing the impact of branding requires a multifaceted approach that considers perception, alignment with values, technological tools, ROI, and DEI initiatives. By systematically evaluating these elements, organizations can ensure that their branding efforts are not only effective in achieving business goals but also in fostering a positive workplace culture that attracts and retains top talent.

Case Studies in Branding Success

Branding success is a multi-faceted achievement that requires a deep understanding of market dynamics, consumer psychology, and strategic foresight. In exploring the case studies of successful branding, we delve into the components that distinguish thriving brands from their less successful counterparts. These case studies offer valuable insights into how companies can effectively use branding to establish a strong market presence and foster consumer loyalty.

One critical element in branding success is the ability to create a compelling narrative that resonates with the target audience. Successful brands often tell a story that connects with consumers on an emotional level, providing not just a product or service, but an experience or a lifestyle. This narrative is not static; it evolves with consumer expectations and cultural trends, ensuring the brand remains relevant over time.

Another significant factor is the consistency of brand messaging across all channels. Successful brands maintain a uniform message that reinforces their core values and promises. This consistency helps to build trust and recognition among consumers, which is crucial for long-term success. Brands that manage to deliver consistent messages across traditional media, digital platforms, and in-store experiences often succeed in creating a cohesive brand image that consumers can easily identify and rely on.

Innovation also plays a pivotal role in branding success. Brands that continuously innovate their products, services, or marketing strategies are more likely to capture consumer interest and differentiate themselves from competitors. Case studies reveal that innovation doesn't necessarily mean reinventing the wheel; rather, it involves finding new ways to meet consumer needs or solve problems more effectively than before.

Moreover, successful branding often involves an element of authenticity. In an era where consumers are increasingly skeptical of marketing gimmicks, authenticity can be a powerful differentiator. Brands that are transparent about their values, practices, and challenges are more likely to earn consumer trust and loyalty. This transparency can be demonstrated through honest advertising, ethical business practices, and a commitment to social responsibility.

The role of consumer engagement cannot be overstated in these case studies. Engaging consumers through interactive campaigns, social media, and personalized experiences creates a sense of community and belonging. This engagement fosters a two-way relationship where consumers feel valued and heard, enhancing their loyalty to the brand.

Finally, adaptability is a hallmark of branding success. The ability to pivot in response to changing market conditions, consumer preferences, or technological advancements is crucial. Brands that are agile and adaptable can quickly respond to challenges and seize new opportunities, ensuring their continued relevance and competitiveness.

In summary, these case studies illuminate the multifaceted nature of branding success. By weaving together a compelling narrative, maintaining consistent messaging, embracing innovation, demonstrating authenticity, engaging consumers, and remaining adaptable, brands can achieve remarkable success in today's competitive marketplace. These elements not only help in establishing a robust brand identity but also in securing a lasting connection with consumers.

Structural Barriers in Career Growth

Identifying Structural Barriers

In the contemporary landscape of human resources and recruitment, the integration of artificial intelligence (AI) offers transformative potential to address deeply ingrained structural barriers. These barriers, often subtle yet pervasive, hinder equitable access to opportunities and fair treatment in professional environments. Through a meticulous examination of these obstacles, organizations can leverage AI to foster a more inclusive workplace.

Structural barriers manifest in various forms, from biased recruitment practices to uneven opportunities for career advancement. These barriers are not always overt; they often exist as implicit biases embedded within organizational processes and decision-making frameworks. For instance, traditional job postings may unconsciously favor certain demographics through the language used, which can deter a diverse range of candidates from applying. AI-powered language analysis tools present a solution by identifying and removing biased wording, thus creating more inclusive job descriptions that appeal to a broader audience.

Beyond recruitment, structural barriers extend into career progression and promotions. Historical data often reveals disparities in how different groups advance within a company. AI can play a crucial role in analyzing these patterns, identifying inequities, and suggesting corrective measures. Predictive analytics, for example, can be employed to ensure that promotion decisions are based on merit rather than being influenced by unconscious bias. By utilizing AI-driven insights, organizations can make more objective assessments of employee performance, reducing the likelihood of biased evaluations.

Another significant area where structural barriers persist is in workplace culture. Resistance to diversity, equity, and inclusion (DEI) initiatives often stems from deeply rooted cultural norms and attitudes. AI-driven sentiment analysis can help organizations detect these internal barriers by analyzing employee communications and feedback. This analysis provides valuable insights into the underlying sentiments that may impede change, allowing leaders to address these issues proactively. Moreover, personalized AI-driven training programs can be developed to equip leaders with the skills necessary to foster an inclusive workplace environment.

The ethical implementation of AI is paramount to ensuring that these technologies do not inadvertently reinforce existing biases. It is crucial for organizations to establish transparent AI audits and maintain human oversight to monitor AI-driven processes. By doing so, they can safeguard against potential biases in AI algorithms and uphold ethical standards in their application. This commitment to transparency and ethical governance is essential for building trust and achieving genuine progress in dismantling structural barriers.

Ultimately, the journey towards identifying and overcoming structural barriers is ongoing and requires a concerted effort from all stakeholders within an organization. By harnessing the capabilities of AI, businesses can create a more equitable and inclusive environment that not only attracts diverse talent but also empowers all employees to thrive.

This transformation is not merely about compliance; it is about fundamentally reshaping the organizational landscape to reflect the values of diversity, equity, and inclusion.

AI in Career Progression Analysis

In the dynamic landscape of modern workplaces, understanding the trajectory of career progression is pivotal for both employees and employers. Artificial Intelligence (AI) has emerged as a transformative tool in analyzing career paths, providing insights that were previously unattainable through traditional methods. By leveraging AI, organizations can dissect complex data to identify patterns and trends in career development, enabling a more equitable and efficient approach to promotions and growth opportunities.

AI tools are adept at processing vast amounts of data, which can reveal subtle biases in career progression that may not be immediately visible. For instance, AI can analyze historical promotion data to uncover disparities that affect specific groups.

This capability allows organizations to address these inequalities proactively, ensuring that career advancement is based on merit rather than unconscious bias or systemic barriers.

Moreover, predictive analytics powered by AI can forecast potential career paths for employees, helping managers make informed decisions about promotions. By evaluating an employee's skills, performance, and potential, AI can suggest career trajectories that align with both personal aspirations and organizational needs. This predictive capability not only aids in fairer promotion decisions but also enhances employee satisfaction by aligning career opportunities with individual goals.

AI also plays a crucial role in refining performance evaluations. Traditionally, these evaluations have been subjective, often influenced by human biases. AI-driven insights can provide a more objective assessment by analyzing performance data against established benchmarks. This objectivity reduces the likelihood of bias in performance reviews, fostering a more transparent and just evaluation process.

Furthermore, the integration of AI into career progression analysis contributes to a culture of continuous improvement. Organizations can use AI to monitor the effectiveness of career development programs and make data-driven adjustments as needed. This ongoing analysis ensures that career progression strategies remain relevant and effective, adapting to the evolving needs of the workforce.

However, the implementation of AI in career progression analysis is not without challenges. It is imperative to ensure that the AI systems themselves are free from bias. This requires a robust framework for developing and auditing AI algorithms to prevent the reinforcement of existing inequalities. Transparency in AI operations and maintaining human oversight are critical to achieving fair and ethical outcomes.

As organizations continue to embrace AI in career progression analysis, they must do so with a commitment to ethical practices. By leveraging AI responsibly, companies can not only enhance career development opportunities but also contribute to a more inclusive and equitable workplace.

The promise of AI in this domain lies in its ability to transform career progression from a subjective art into a data-driven science, enabling organizations to unlock the full potential of their workforce.

Predictive Analytics for Promotions

Predictive analytics is transforming the landscape of promotions within organizations by offering data-driven insights that enable fairer and more objective decision-making processes. By leveraging historical data and advanced algorithms, predictive analytics can forecast potential future outcomes, thus allowing companies to refine their promotion strategies and reduce bias.

At its core, predictive analytics involves the use of statistical techniques and machine learning to analyze current and historical data to make predictions about future events. In the context of promotions, this means assessing an employee's past performance, skills, and career trajectory to predict their suitability for advancement. This approach helps in mitigating the subjective biases that often plague traditional promotion processes.

One of the key benefits of using predictive analytics for promotions is its ability to identify patterns and correlations that might not be immediately obvious to human evaluators. For instance, it can highlight the competencies and behaviors that are most strongly correlated with success in higher roles, allowing organizations to tailor their development programs accordingly. This ensures that employees who are truly deserving of promotion are recognized, rather than those who may simply be more vocal or visible.

Moreover, predictive analytics can support diversity and inclusion initiatives by pinpointing potential disparities in promotion practices. By analyzing demographic data alongside performance metrics, organizations can identify whether certain groups are being systematically overlooked for promotions and take corrective actions. This data-driven approach not only fosters a more equitable workplace but also enhances the overall organizational culture by promoting fairness and transparency.

The implementation of predictive analytics in promotions also requires careful consideration of ethical and privacy concerns. Organizations must ensure that the data used is accurate, relevant, and collected in a manner that respects employee privacy. Additionally, the algorithms employed should be transparent and regularly audited to prevent the reinforcement of existing biases. This involves a commitment to continuous monitoring and adjustment of the predictive models to align with the organization's values and diversity goals.

As organizations increasingly turn to predictive analytics to guide their promotion decisions, it is crucial to integrate these tools within a broader strategic framework. This includes aligning predictive analytics capabilities with the organization's overall talent management strategy and ensuring that all stakeholders are trained to understand and utilize these insights effectively. By doing so, companies can enhance their ability to promote the right individuals while maintaining a commitment to ethical and inclusive practices.

In conclusion, predictive analytics offers a powerful means to transform promotion processes within organizations. By providing objective, data-driven insights, it helps reduce biases, supports diversity, and ensures that promotions are based on merit rather than subjective judgment. As organizations continue to navigate the complexities of modern workforce management, predictive analytics will undoubtedly play an increasingly pivotal role in shaping fairer and more effective promotional strategies.

Reducing Bias in Evaluations

Evaluating performance in the workplace is a critical process that influences career progression and remuneration. However, these evaluations are often marred by biases, both conscious and unconscious, which can skew results and perpetuate inequalities. To address this, it is essential to implement measures that can reduce bias in evaluations, ensuring a fair and equitable assessment of employee performance.

One effective approach to reducing bias in evaluations is the integration of artificial intelligence (AI) tools that offer data-driven insights. These tools can analyze performance data objectively, identifying patterns and trends that might be overlooked by human evaluators. By relying on AI for initial data collection and analysis, organizations can minimize the impact of subjective judgments and personal biases.

AI can highlight discrepancies in evaluations across different demographic groups, thus providing a basis for more informed decision-making.

Moreover, it is crucial to establish clear criteria for performance evaluations that are aligned with organizational goals and values. These criteria should be communicated transparently to all employees, ensuring that everyone understands what is expected from them and how their performance will be measured. This transparency helps to mitigate bias by providing a standardized framework for evaluations, reducing the room for subjective interpretation.

Training evaluators is another vital step in reducing bias. Organizations must invest in training programs that raise awareness about different types of biases, such as gender, racial, and confirmation biases, and teach evaluators how to recognize and counteract these biases in their assessments. This training should be ongoing, reinforcing the importance of unbiased evaluations and equipping evaluators with the skills needed to conduct fair assessments.

Feedback mechanisms play a pivotal role in reducing bias as well. Implementing a structured feedback process that invites input from multiple sources can provide a more rounded view of an employee's performance. This 360-degree feedback approach incorporates perspectives from peers, subordinates, and supervisors, thereby diluting the influence of any one individual's bias. Additionally, encouraging self-assessment allows employees to reflect on their own performance, fostering a culture of self-improvement and accountability.

Another strategy involves conducting regular audits of evaluation processes and outcomes. These audits should examine whether certain groups consistently receive lower evaluations and, if so, investigate potential causes. By identifying patterns of bias, organizations can take corrective actions, such as revising evaluation criteria or retraining evaluators. Audits also demonstrate a commitment to fairness and can help build trust among employees.

Finally, fostering an inclusive organizational culture can help mitigate bias in evaluations. When diversity and inclusion are prioritized, employees are more likely to feel valued and respected, reducing the likelihood of bias influencing evaluations. Organizations should promote diversity at all levels, ensuring that evaluators themselves come from diverse backgrounds and can bring varied perspectives to the evaluation process.

In summary, reducing bias in evaluations requires a multi-faceted approach that combines technology, training, transparency, and cultural change. By implementing these strategies, organizations can create a more equitable evaluation process that recognizes and rewards genuine performance, ultimately contributing to a fairer and more inclusive workplace.

Implementing Fair Practices

Implementing fair practices in the realm of AI-driven hiring and employer branding requires a meticulous approach to ensure that the technology serves as a tool for equity rather than perpetuating existing biases. One fundamental aspect is the development of a comprehensive framework that guides the ethical use of AI in these processes. This involves setting clear guidelines and standards that define what fair practices look like in the context of AI usage.

To begin with, understanding the intricacies of AI algorithms is crucial. These algorithms, if not carefully managed, can inadvertently replicate the biases present in the data they are trained on. Therefore, it is essential to ensure that the data sets used are diverse and representative of the population. This requires a concerted effort to audit data for any inherent biases and to continuously update these data sets to reflect current realities.

Another key element is transparency. Organizations must be open about the AI tools they use and the decision-making processes these tools support. This transparency builds trust among stakeholders and allows for external audits and feedback, which are invaluable for continuous improvement. Transparency also involves clear communication with candidates about how AI is being used in the recruitment process, including how decisions are made and what data is being utilized.

Human oversight remains a critical component in implementing fair practices. While AI can process vast amounts of data more quickly than humans, it lacks the nuanced understanding of context and empathy that human judgment provides. Therefore, combining AI with human decision-making can help mitigate potential errors and biases.

This hybrid approach ensures that AI serves as an aid to human recruiters and HR professionals rather than a replacement.

Additionally, the implementation of fair practices involves ongoing education and training for those involved in the hiring and branding processes. This training should focus on the ethical use of AI, the recognition of bias, and strategies for promoting inclusivity. By equipping HR professionals with the knowledge and skills needed to oversee AI-driven processes, organizations can better ensure that these technologies are used responsibly and effectively.

Furthermore, regular audits and evaluations of AI systems are necessary to identify any emerging biases or unintended consequences. These evaluations should be conducted by independent bodies to ensure objectivity and credibility. The findings can then inform adjustments and improvements to the AI systems, ensuring they remain aligned with the organization's fairness and inclusivity goals.

Incorporating stakeholder feedback is another crucial aspect of implementing fair practices. Engaging with employees, candidates, and other stakeholders provides valuable insights into their experiences and perceptions of the AI-driven processes. This feedback can highlight areas for improvement and help organizations refine their approaches to ensure fairness and equity.

Ultimately, implementing fair practices in AI-driven hiring and employer branding is an ongoing journey that requires commitment, vigilance, and a willingness to adapt. By prioritizing fairness, transparency, and human oversight, organizations can harness the power of AI to create more equitable and inclusive workplaces.

AI-Driven Workplace Culture

Measuring Workplace Sentiment

In the contemporary business landscape, understanding employee sentiment has become a cornerstone for fostering a productive and inclusive workplace. The advent of artificial intelligence (AI) has revolutionized the way organizations can gauge and interpret the emotions and attitudes of their workforce. AI-driven sentiment analysis tools offer a nuanced approach to capturing the pulse of an organization, providing insights that were previously difficult to obtain.

Sentiment analysis in the workplace involves the use of natural language processing (NLP) to analyze text data from various sources such as emails, chat messages, surveys, and social media. This technology allows companies to assess the overall mood and satisfaction of employees, identify potential issues, and understand the impact of organizational changes. By analyzing language patterns, tone, and frequency of certain keywords, AI can generate a comprehensive picture of employee sentiment.

One of the primary benefits of using AI for sentiment analysis is its ability to process large volumes of data quickly and accurately. Traditional methods of gauging employee sentiment often relied on periodic surveys and feedback forms, which could be time-consuming and limited in scope. AI, on the other hand, can continuously monitor sentiment in real-time, providing organizations with up-to-date insights that enable proactive management of workplace issues.

Furthermore, AI-driven sentiment analysis helps in identifying underlying issues that may not be immediately apparent. For instance, it can detect subtle shifts in mood across different departments or teams, which might indicate brewing dissatisfaction or conflict. By addressing these issues early, organizations can prevent them from escalating into more significant problems that could affect productivity or employee retention.

Another critical aspect of workplace sentiment analysis is its role in promoting diversity, equity, and inclusion (DEI).

AI tools can uncover biases in communication patterns, helping organizations to identify and address structural barriers that may hinder the progress of underrepresented groups. By fostering an inclusive environment where all employees feel heard and valued, companies can enhance employee engagement and satisfaction.

However, the implementation of AI in measuring workplace sentiment is not without challenges. Concerns about privacy and data security are paramount, as employees may be wary of having their communications monitored. It is essential for organizations to establish clear policies and ethical guidelines to ensure transparency and trust. Additionally, AI algorithms must be designed to minimize bias and provide fair and accurate assessments of sentiment.

In conclusion, AI-driven sentiment analysis is a powerful tool for understanding and improving workplace dynamics. It offers organizations the ability to make informed decisions based on real-time data, ultimately leading to a more engaged and satisfied workforce. As AI technology continues to evolve, its application in measuring workplace sentiment will undoubtedly become more sophisticated, providing even deeper insights into the complexities of human emotions and interactions in the workplace.

AI for Inclusive Leadership Training

Artificial Intelligence (AI) serves as a transformative tool in fostering inclusive leadership training, providing an innovative approach to addressing the challenges of diversity, equity, and inclusion (DEI) in organizational environments. By leveraging AI, organizations can develop more effective strategies for cultivating leaders who are both aware of and sensitive to the diverse needs of their teams. AI's capacity to process vast amounts of data allows it to identify patterns of bias and exclusion that may not be immediately apparent to human observers. This ability is crucial in creating training programs that are not only comprehensive but also tailored to the specific dynamics of each organization.

One of the primary benefits of AI in inclusive leadership training is its ability to customize learning experiences. AI can analyze individual learning styles and preferences, adapting training modules to suit each leader's unique needs. This personalization ensures that leaders are engaged and can absorb the material more effectively, leading to a deeper understanding of inclusive practices. Furthermore, AI can continuously update these training programs based on new data and feedback, ensuring that the content remains relevant and effective in addressing current DEI challenges.

AI also plays a significant role in facilitating self-awareness and reflection among leaders. Through AI-driven assessments and simulations, leaders can gain insights into their own biases and how these may impact their decision-making processes. These tools provide a safe space for leaders to explore and understand their unconscious biases without fear of judgment, encouraging honest reflection and growth. By confronting these biases, leaders are better equipped to foster an inclusive environment that values and respects diversity.

Moreover, AI enhances the scalability of inclusive leadership training. Traditional training programs often require significant resources and time, limiting their reach and impact. In contrast, AI-driven programs can be deployed across multiple locations and adapted to different cultural contexts, making them accessible to a broader range of leaders. This scalability ensures that organizations can implement inclusive practices more widely and consistently, promoting a culture of inclusivity at all levels.

In addition to personalizing and scaling training programs, AI can also provide valuable insights into the effectiveness of these initiatives. By analyzing data on participant engagement and performance, AI can identify which aspects of the training are most beneficial and which areas require improvement. This data-driven approach allows organizations to refine their training programs continuously, ensuring they remain effective in promoting inclusive leadership.

While AI offers numerous advantages in inclusive leadership training, it is essential to approach its implementation with caution. Organizations must ensure that the AI systems they use are designed and operated ethically, with safeguards in place to prevent the reinforcement of existing biases. Transparent AI audits and human oversight are critical in maintaining the integrity of these systems and ensuring they contribute positively to DEI efforts.

Overall, AI provides a powerful tool for enhancing inclusive leadership training, offering personalized, scalable, and data-driven solutions to the challenges of diversity and inclusion in the workplace. By harnessing the potential of AI, organizations can develop leaders who are not only aware of their biases but also equipped to create inclusive environments that celebrate diversity and foster equity.

Anonymous Feedback and Reporting

In the realm of organizational dynamics, the mechanisms for gathering anonymous feedback and ensuring comprehensive reporting are pivotal in fostering a culture of inclusivity and transparency. These systems allow employees to voice their concerns without fear of retribution, thus enabling organizations to identify and mitigate issues that might otherwise remain hidden. The advent of AI has significantly transformed how feedback is collected and processed, offering new avenues for ensuring that every voice is heard and valued.

Anonymous feedback systems, when effectively implemented, serve as a vital tool for capturing the authentic sentiments of the workforce. They allow employees to express their thoughts on workplace practices, leadership decisions, and overall organizational culture without the fear of being singled out or judged. This anonymity is crucial in obtaining honest and unfiltered feedback, which is indispensable for genuine organizational improvement. AI technology enhances this process by efficiently sorting through large volumes of feedback, identifying key themes, and highlighting areas that require immediate attention.

AI-powered tools can analyze feedback data to detect patterns and trends that might not be immediately apparent to human analysts. For instance, sentiment analysis algorithms can gauge the emotional tone of feedback, offering insights into the overall morale and engagement levels within the organization. By categorizing feedback into actionable insights, AI helps leaders understand the underlying causes of dissatisfaction or disengagement, thereby facilitating targeted interventions.

Moreover, AI-driven feedback systems can be designed to ensure that feedback is not only collected but also acted upon. This involves integrating feedback mechanisms with reporting tools that provide detailed analytics on the types of issues being reported, the frequency of specific complaints, and the demographics of the employees providing feedback. Such comprehensive reporting enables organizations to track the efficacy of their diversity, equity, and inclusion (DEI) initiatives, ensuring that they are not merely performative but lead to tangible improvements.

The role of AI in anonymous feedback and reporting also extends to safeguarding the integrity and confidentiality of the feedback process. Advanced encryption and data protection measures ensure that employees' identities remain confidential, thereby encouraging more candid participation. Additionally, AI can help in distinguishing between constructive feedback and malicious or unfounded complaints, thus maintaining the credibility of the feedback system.

However, the reliance on AI for feedback and reporting is not without challenges. There is a risk that biases inherent in AI algorithms could skew the analysis or interpretation of feedback data. Therefore, it is essential for organizations to regularly audit their AI systems to ensure fairness and accuracy in feedback processing. Transparency in how feedback data is handled and reported is also crucial in building trust among employees.

In conclusion, anonymous feedback and reporting systems, augmented by AI, are indispensable for nurturing an inclusive and responsive workplace culture. They empower employees to contribute to organizational growth and innovation while ensuring that their concerns are addressed in a timely and effective manner. As organizations continue to navigate the complexities of modern work environments, these systems will play a critical role in shaping a future where every employee feels heard and valued.

Overcoming Resistance to DEI

To effectively address and overcome resistance to Diversity, Equity, and Inclusion (DEI) initiatives, it is crucial to understand the underlying factors contributing to this resistance. Often, resistance stems from a lack of awareness or understanding of DEI's benefits, fear of change, or perceived threats to personal or group interests. Therefore, an essential first step is education and communication. Providing clear, evidence-based information about the advantages of a diverse and inclusive workplace can help mitigate fears and misconceptions. This involves presenting data that demonstrates how DEI initiatives lead to improved employee satisfaction, innovation, and financial performance.

Engaging leadership is another critical component in overcoming resistance. Leaders must not only support DEI initiatives but also actively participate in them. This involvement signals to the entire organization the importance of these efforts. Leaders can model inclusive behavior, ensuring that DEI becomes an integral part of the company culture rather than an isolated program. Training programs focused on developing inclusive leadership skills can equip leaders with the tools they need to foster an environment where diversity is valued.

The role of AI in overcoming resistance to DEI cannot be overstated. AI can help identify and eliminate biases in recruitment, promotions, and performance evaluations. By automating these processes, AI reduces the likelihood of unconscious biases influencing decision-making. However, it is essential to ensure that AI systems themselves are designed and implemented ethically and transparently to prevent the reinforcement of existing biases. Regular audits and updates of AI systems can help maintain their fairness and effectiveness.

Creating a safe space for dialogue is also vital. Employees should feel comfortable expressing their concerns and experiences without fear of retribution. Anonymous feedback mechanisms and regular DEI surveys can provide valuable insights into the organization's climate and highlight areas needing improvement. This feedback loop enables continuous adaptation and enhancement of DEI strategies.

Another effective strategy is to personalize DEI initiatives. Recognizing that different groups may face unique challenges and barriers allows for more targeted interventions. Tailored training programs, mentorship opportunities, and employee resource groups can provide support and foster a sense of belonging among diverse employees.

Finally, measuring the impact of DEI initiatives is essential for demonstrating their value and gaining buy-in from skeptics. Establishing clear metrics and regularly reporting on progress can help maintain momentum and accountability. This transparency reassures stakeholders that DEI efforts are not just performative but are leading to tangible improvements within the organization.

By addressing resistance through education, leadership engagement, ethical AI use, open dialogue, personalized initiatives, and measurable outcomes, organizations can create a more inclusive and equitable workplace. This comprehensive approach not only helps overcome resistance but also ensures the sustainability and success of DEI initiatives.

Building a Culture of Inclusion

Building a culture of inclusion within an organization involves intentional and strategic efforts to create an environment where diversity is genuinely valued and every individual feels that they belong. This process starts with understanding the current organizational culture and identifying the areas where inclusivity is lacking. Leaders must be committed to fostering an inclusive environment, which can be achieved by setting clear goals, providing resources, and regularly assessing progress.

An inclusive culture does not happen by chance; it requires deliberate actions and policies that promote diversity and equity. Organizations must develop comprehensive diversity and inclusion (D&I) strategies that encompass recruitment, training, and employee engagement. These strategies should be integrated into the organization's core values and operations, ensuring that inclusion is not just a peripheral activity but a fundamental aspect of the business.

Training and education play a crucial role in building a culture of inclusion. Employees at all levels should be educated about the importance of diversity and inclusion, as well as the benefits it brings to the organization. Training programs should aim to raise awareness about unconscious biases and provide tools to mitigate them. Additionally, promoting cultural competence and sensitivity among employees can enhance interactions and understanding within diverse teams.

Leadership is critical in driving a culture of inclusion. Leaders must model inclusive behavior and hold themselves accountable for promoting diversity within their teams. They should actively listen to employees' concerns and feedback, using this information to make informed decisions that enhance inclusivity. Moreover, leaders should ensure that diversity and inclusion are prioritized in strategic planning and decision-making processes.

Creating inclusive policies and practices is another essential component. Organizations should review their policies to identify any that may inadvertently exclude certain groups. This includes examining recruitment processes, performance evaluations, and promotion criteria to ensure they are fair and equitable. Implementing flexible work arrangements and providing support for diverse needs, such as parental leave and disability accommodations, can also contribute to a more inclusive workplace.

Employee resource groups (ERGs) and diversity councils can be valuable tools in promoting a culture of inclusion. These groups provide a platform for employees to connect, share experiences, and advocate for change. ERGs can also offer insights into the unique challenges faced by different employee groups and propose solutions to address them.

Measuring the impact of inclusion efforts is vital to understand what is working and what needs improvement. Organizations should establish metrics to assess the effectiveness of their D&I initiatives, such as employee satisfaction surveys, diversity demographics, and retention rates. Regularly reviewing these metrics can help organizations identify trends and make necessary adjustments to their strategies.

In summary, building a culture of inclusion requires a comprehensive approach that involves commitment from leadership, strategic planning, and continuous evaluation.

By embedding inclusivity into the organizational fabric, companies can create a more dynamic, innovative, and equitable workplace that benefits everyone.

Ensuring AI Fairness and Transparency

Best Practices for AI Fairness

In the rapidly evolving landscape of artificial intelligence, ensuring fairness in AI systems is paramount. The potential for AI to revolutionize industries is immense, but with this power comes the responsibility to prevent the perpetuation of existing biases. As AI becomes increasingly integrated into decision-making processes, particularly in sensitive areas like hiring and talent management, the stakes are high. Therefore, establishing best practices for AI fairness is not just a technical challenge but an ethical imperative.

One of the foundational steps in promoting AI fairness is recognizing and mitigating bias in data. AI systems learn from the data they are trained on, which means that any biases present in the data can be inadvertently amplified by the AI. To counteract this, it is crucial to implement rigorous data auditing processes. This involves scrutinizing data sources for representativeness and ensuring that the data reflects diverse demographics and perspectives. Techniques such as re-sampling, re-weighting, and synthetic data generation can be employed to balance datasets and reduce bias.

Another critical practice is the development of transparent AI models. Transparency in AI involves making the decision-making processes of AI systems understandable to humans. This can be achieved through the use of interpretable models and providing explanations for AI decisions. By doing so, stakeholders can better understand how and why certain decisions are made, which is essential for identifying and addressing potential biases. Moreover, transparency fosters trust in AI systems, which is vital for their acceptance and adoption.

Human oversight is also a key component of AI fairness. While AI can process vast amounts of data and identify patterns beyond human capability, it is not infallible. Incorporating human judgment into AI-driven processes ensures that decisions are not solely reliant on algorithmic outputs. This can take the form of human-in-the-loop systems, where human experts review and validate AI decisions, particularly in high-stakes scenarios. Such oversight acts as a safeguard against erroneous or biased AI outputs.

Regular auditing and monitoring of AI systems are essential to maintain fairness over time. As AI systems are deployed and interact with real-world data, their performance and fairness levels may change. Continuous monitoring allows for the detection of any drift in model behavior or emergence of new biases. Audits should be conducted periodically to assess the fairness and accuracy of AI systems, and adjustments should be made as necessary to align with ethical standards.

Lastly, fostering a culture of accountability and ethical responsibility within organizations is crucial for upholding AI fairness. This involves establishing clear guidelines and ethical frameworks for AI development and deployment. Organizations should prioritize ethics training for AI developers and stakeholders to ensure that fairness is a core consideration throughout the AI lifecycle. Additionally, engaging with diverse groups and incorporating their feedback can provide valuable insights into potential biases and fairness issues.

In summary, best practices for AI fairness involve a multi-faceted approach that includes data auditing, transparency, human oversight, continuous monitoring, and organizational accountability. By implementing these practices, we can harness the power of AI while safeguarding against the reinforcement of existing inequalities.

The Importance of AI Audits

The increasing integration of artificial intelligence (AI) in various sectors, particularly in human resources, necessitates a comprehensive understanding of its implications. AI audits emerge as a crucial practice in ensuring that these systems are not only efficient but also ethical and unbiased. As AI continues to shape the landscape of hiring and employer branding, the importance of scrutinizing these systems cannot be overstated.

AI audits serve as a vital mechanism to evaluate the fairness and transparency of AI systems. They involve assessing the algorithms and data sets used in AI applications to identify potential biases or ethical concerns. This process is essential because AI systems, if left unchecked, can perpetuate existing societal biases. By conducting regular audits, organizations can ensure that their AI tools promote equality and do not disadvantage any group.

The role of AI audits extends beyond merely identifying biases. They provide a framework for accountability and transparency, fostering trust among stakeholders. When organizations commit to AI audits, they demonstrate a dedication to ethical practices and a willingness to be held accountable for their AI systems' outcomes. This transparency is crucial in building confidence among employees and candidates, who may otherwise be skeptical of AI-driven decisions.

Moreover, AI audits can guide improvements in AI systems. By highlighting areas where biases may exist, these audits offer insights into how algorithms can be refined to ensure fairer outcomes. This iterative process of auditing and refining not only enhances the performance of AI systems but also contributes to the broader goal of ethical AI deployment across industries.

In the context of hiring and employer branding, AI audits are particularly significant. These areas are highly susceptible to bias, given the subjective nature of recruitment and the potential for AI to reinforce existing inequalities. Through audits, organizations can scrutinize their AI-driven hiring practices, ensuring that candidate selection processes are based on merit and are free from discriminatory practices.

Furthermore, AI audits can inform policy development within organizations. By understanding the biases inherent in AI systems, companies can develop more robust policies that address these issues proactively. This proactive stance is crucial in a rapidly evolving technological landscape, where regulatory frameworks may lag behind technological advancements.

In essence, AI audits are not merely a technical exercise but a strategic one. They align with the broader organizational goals of diversity, equity, and inclusion, ensuring that AI systems contribute positively to these objectives. As AI continues to evolve, the need for rigorous and regular audits will only grow, underscoring their importance in navigating the complexities of AI ethics and bias mitigation.

Human Oversight in AI Systems

Human oversight in AI systems is crucial to ensure that these technologies operate within ethical boundaries and align with human values. As AI systems become more integrated into decision-making processes, particularly in sensitive areas such as hiring, it is imperative to maintain a balance between automation and human judgment. This balance helps prevent AI from perpetuating biases and ensures decisions are made with a comprehensive understanding of context and implications.

The role of human oversight begins with the design and development of AI systems. Designers must incorporate ethical considerations from the outset, ensuring that AI tools are transparent and their decision-making processes can be audited. This transparency is vital for identifying biases that may be embedded in the algorithms or data sets used by AI systems. Developers should work closely with ethicists and domain experts to create AI systems that are not only effective but also fair and just.

Once deployed, AI systems require continuous monitoring to ensure they function as intended. Human oversight involves regularly reviewing AI outputs and decisions to identify any discrepancies or biases that may have arisen. This process includes auditing AI systems to ensure they conform to established ethical standards and regulatory requirements. By doing so, organizations can maintain trust in their AI systems and demonstrate a commitment to ethical practices.

Training and education are also essential components of human oversight in AI systems. Stakeholders, including HR professionals and decision-makers, must be equipped with the knowledge and skills to understand AI outputs and question them when necessary. This education fosters a culture of accountability, where humans remain the ultimate decision-makers and are responsible for the outcomes of AI-driven processes. By understanding the limitations of AI, humans can intervene when systems operate outside their intended scope or when ethical dilemmas arise.

Moreover, human oversight is crucial for addressing the limitations of AI in understanding nuanced human contexts. AI systems can process vast amounts of data and identify patterns, but they lack the ability to comprehend the subtleties of human interactions and emotions fully. Human oversight ensures that decisions made by AI systems are contextualized and adjusted based on human insights, thus preventing potential misinterpretations or harmful outcomes.

Incorporating human oversight in AI systems also involves establishing feedback mechanisms where users can report issues or biases they observe. This feedback is valuable for continuously improving AI systems and ensuring they evolve to meet ethical standards. It encourages a collaborative approach where humans and AI work together to achieve better outcomes.

As AI continues to evolve, the importance of human oversight will only grow. It is a critical component in ensuring that AI systems enhance human capabilities rather than undermine them. By integrating human oversight into AI systems, organizations can harness the benefits of AI while safeguarding against its potential risks, thus paving the way for a more equitable and ethical future in AI-driven decision-making.

Regulatory Considerations

In the landscape of AI-driven human resources, regulatory considerations play a pivotal role in ensuring that technology is used ethically and responsibly. The integration of AI into HR processes, particularly in hiring and employer branding, necessitates a thorough understanding of existing regulations and a proactive approach to compliance. As organizations increasingly rely on AI to drive efficiency and fairness, it becomes crucial to align these technologies with legal and ethical standards.

One of the primary regulatory concerns is data privacy. AI systems in HR often require access to vast amounts of personal data to function effectively. Regulations such as the General Data Protection Regulation (GDPR) in Europe set stringent requirements for data handling, ensuring that personal information is processed lawfully, transparently, and for legitimate purposes. Organizations must implement robust data protection measures to comply with these regulations, safeguarding employee and candidate information from unauthorized access or misuse.

Another critical aspect is the prevention of bias and discrimination. While AI has the potential to minimize human biases in recruitment, it can also perpetuate or even exacerbate existing biases if not carefully managed. Regulatory frameworks are evolving to address these challenges, emphasizing the need for transparency and accountability in AI algorithms. Regular audits and assessments of AI systems are necessary to ensure they operate fairly and do not discriminate based on protected characteristics such as gender, race, or age.

Transparency is also a key regulatory consideration. Stakeholders, including job applicants and employees, have the right to understand how AI decisions are made and what data is being used. Clear communication about the role of AI in decision-making processes helps build trust and ensures compliance with transparency requirements. This includes providing explanations for AI-driven decisions and maintaining documentation that can be reviewed by regulatory bodies if needed.

Additionally, human oversight remains an essential factor in the regulatory landscape. While AI can enhance decision-making, human judgment should not be entirely replaced. Regulatory guidelines often stress the importance of human involvement to validate and interpret AI outcomes, ensuring that decisions align with ethical standards and organizational values.

As AI technologies continue to evolve, so too will the regulatory environment. Organizations must stay informed about changes in legislation and best practices to remain compliant. This involves continuous education and training for HR professionals to understand the implications of AI in their field and to develop strategies that align with both technological advancements and regulatory requirements.

In summary, regulatory considerations in AI-driven HR are multifaceted, encompassing data privacy, bias prevention, transparency, and human oversight. By adhering to these principles, organizations can harness the benefits of AI while upholding ethical standards and fostering a fair and inclusive workplace. The path forward requires a balanced approach that respects both technological innovation and regulatory compliance, ensuring that AI serves as a tool for positive change in the realm of human resources.

Ethical Frameworks for AI

In the rapidly evolving landscape of artificial intelligence, the integration of ethical frameworks is not just a necessity but a responsibility that shapes the future of technology and society. As AI systems increasingly permeate various sectors, from healthcare to finance, the ethical considerations underlying their deployment become paramount. These frameworks serve as guiding principles that ensure AI technologies are developed and utilized in ways that align with human values, promoting fairness, accountability, and transparency.

One of the fundamental aspects of ethical frameworks for AI is the commitment to fairness. This involves designing algorithms that do not perpetuate existing biases or create new ones. Fairness in AI is achieved by ensuring that datasets used to train AI models are representative of diverse populations, thereby reducing the risk of biased outcomes. Moreover, it includes implementing mechanisms that continuously monitor AI systems for discriminatory behavior, allowing for timely interventions and corrections.

Transparency is another critical pillar of ethical AI. It demands that AI systems are not black boxes but rather open and understandable to those who deploy, regulate, and are affected by them. Transparency involves clear documentation of AI decision-making processes, enabling stakeholders to comprehend how decisions are made and on what basis. This level of openness not only builds trust among users but also facilitates accountability, as it allows for the examination and auditing of AI systems by independent bodies.

Accountability in AI requires that there are clear lines of responsibility for the outcomes produced by AI systems. Organizations implementing AI need to establish governance structures that define who is accountable for the ethical deployment of AI technologies. This includes creating roles such as AI ethics officers and committees dedicated to overseeing the ethical implications of AI initiatives. Furthermore, accountability involves setting up protocols for redress in cases where AI systems cause harm or produce unfair outcomes.

The ethical use of AI also emphasizes the importance of privacy and data protection. As AI systems often rely on vast amounts of personal data, safeguarding this information is crucial to maintaining public trust. Ethical frameworks advocate for robust data protection measures, ensuring that data is collected, stored, and used in compliance with privacy laws and regulations. This includes obtaining informed consent from individuals whose data is being used and implementing technologies that enhance data security, such as encryption and anonymization.

Finally, ethical frameworks for AI underscore the necessity of inclusivity and stakeholder engagement in the AI lifecycle. This involves actively involving diverse groups in the design, development, and deployment of AI technologies to ensure that they cater to a wide range of needs and perspectives. Inclusivity helps in identifying potential biases and ethical issues early in the development process and ensures that AI systems are designed to benefit all segments of society.

In conclusion, ethical frameworks for AI are indispensable for guiding the responsible development and deployment of AI technologies. By adhering to principles of fairness, transparency, accountability, privacy, and inclusivity, these frameworks help ensure that AI acts as a force for good, enhancing human capabilities while safeguarding fundamental human rights.

AI in Talent Attraction

Skills-Based Hiring

In recent years, the landscape of hiring has undergone significant transformations. Among these, skills-based hiring has emerged as a pivotal approach that shifts the focus from traditional credentials to the actual skills and competencies required for a job. This paradigm change is driven by the increasing recognition that traditional hiring methods, often centered around academic qualifications and previous job titles, do not always correlate with job performance or potential for growth within a company.

Skills-based hiring prioritizes an applicant's abilities and practical knowledge over where they went to school or their last job title. This method seeks to identify candidates who possess the necessary skills to perform a given role effectively, regardless of their educational background or work history. By focusing on skills, employers can access a broader talent pool, including individuals who may have non-linear career paths, self-taught skills, or experience gained outside of conventional professional environments.

The adoption of skills-based hiring is supported by various tools and technologies that facilitate the identification and assessment of relevant skills. For instance, AI-driven platforms can analyze a candidate's skill set through various assessments, simulations, and work samples. These technologies help eliminate bias by focusing strictly on the capabilities demonstrated by the candidate, rather than the potentially biased interpretations of their educational or professional pedigree.

Moreover, skills-based hiring can promote diversity and inclusion within organizations. Traditional hiring practices often inadvertently favor candidates from certain educational institutions or backgrounds, which can perpetuate homogeneity within teams. By removing these barriers, skills-based hiring enables companies to tap into diverse talent pools, bringing in varied perspectives that can drive innovation and creativity.

Implementing skills-based hiring requires a cultural shift within organizations. It necessitates rethinking job descriptions to clearly define the skills and competencies required for success in the role. Employers must also invest in training hiring managers and HR professionals to evaluate candidates based on skills assessments rather than relying on resumes as the primary screening tool.

One of the challenges in adopting skills-based hiring is the need for comprehensive skills assessment frameworks. These frameworks should be tailored to the specific needs of the organization and the roles in question. They must be robust enough to accurately gauge a candidate's abilities while being flexible enough to adapt to the evolving demands of the job market.

Furthermore, organizations must ensure that their skills-based hiring processes are transparent and fair. This involves setting clear criteria for skills assessments and providing candidates with feedback on their performance. Transparency in the hiring process not only enhances the candidate experience but also builds trust in the organization's commitment to fair hiring practices.

In conclusion, skills-based hiring represents a forward-thinking approach to talent acquisition that aligns with the needs of modern workplaces. By valuing skills over traditional credentials, organizations can build more capable, diverse, and innovative teams. As this approach continues to gain traction, it has the potential to redefine the future of work, making it more inclusive and merito-cratic.

Enhancing Diversity through AI

Artificial intelligence is increasingly being utilized to pro-mote diversity within organizations. As a tool, AI has the potential to transform recruitment and workplace dy-namics by identifying and mitigating biases that are often embedded in human decision-making processes. By lever-aging AI, companies can ensure a more equitable environ-ment that values diverse perspectives and talents.

One of the primary ways AI enhances diversity is through the improvement of job postings and employer branding. AI-powered language analysis tools can scan job descrip-tions to identify and remove biased wording, which might deter diverse candidates from applying. By fostering neu-tral and inclusive language, organizations can attract a wider pool of applicants, thereby increasing the diversity of their talent pipeline. This process not only helps in creating a more inclusive recruitment material but also ensures that employer branding messages resonate with a broader audience, reflecting the company's commitment to diversity and inclusion.

Moreover, AI is instrumental in addressing structural barriers that hinder career growth and promotion opportunities for underrepresented groups. Through analyzing career progression data, AI can help identify patterns of disparity and suggest interventions to ensure fairer promotion decisions. Predictive analytics can be employed to evaluate performance data more objectively, reducing the influence of unconscious bias in performance evaluations. This ensures that promotions and career advancement are based on merit and potential rather than subjective judgments, thereby fostering an equitable workplace environment.

AI also plays a crucial role in measuring and transforming workplace culture. Sentiment analysis tools can be used to gauge employee perceptions and detect internal barriers to diversity, equity, and inclusion (DEI). By providing insights into employee sentiments, organizations can tailor their DEI strategies to address specific issues, creating a more inclusive workplace culture. Additionally, AI-driven personalized training programs for leadership can enhance inclusivity by equipping leaders with the necessary skills to manage diverse teams effectively.

However, the implementation of AI in promoting diversity is not without challenges. It is imperative to ensure that AI systems themselves are fair, ethical, and transparent. This involves establishing best practices to prevent AI from perpetuating existing biases. Transparent AI audits and the inclusion of human oversight are critical in maintaining the integrity of AI applications in HR processes. Regulatory and ethical considerations must also be taken into account to safeguard against potential biases in AI algorithms.

In the context of hiring and employer branding, AI offers a promising future by shifting organizations from merely talking about diversity to taking tangible actions. By facilitating talent attraction, skills-based hiring, and culture fit assessments, AI can help organizations build more inclusive workplaces.

The potential of AI extends beyond just hiring; it can drive comprehensive workplace inclusion initiatives, ensuring that diversity is not only a metric to be achieved but a fundamental aspect of organizational culture.

AI Tools for Talent Matching

Artificial Intelligence (AI) is revolutionizing the landscape of talent acquisition and management. Its application in talent matching is particularly transformative, offering a blend of efficiency and precision that traditional methods cannot match. At its core, AI-driven talent matching utilizes algorithms that analyze vast amounts of data to identify the best candidates for specific roles. This process involves evaluating candidates' skills, experiences, and potential cultural fit within an organization. By leveraging machine learning models, AI tools can predict which candidates will excel in a given position, thereby streamlining the recruitment process and enhancing decision-making.

One of the most significant advantages of AI in talent matching is its ability to process and analyze large datasets quickly. This capability allows organizations to sift through resumes and candidate profiles with unprecedented speed and accuracy. AI tools can scan for specific keywords, qualifications, and experiences that align with job requirements, effectively narrowing down applicant pools to the most suitable candidates. This not only saves time but also reduces the likelihood of human error and bias that can occur during manual resume screening.

Moreover, AI tools are designed to learn and improve over time. With each recruitment cycle, these systems become more adept at identifying the traits and qualifications that lead to successful hires. This continuous learning process enhances the precision of talent matching, as AI systems refine their algorithms based on past outcomes and feedback. Consequently, organizations can expect a higher quality of hire, which translates to increased productivity and reduced turnover rates.

Another critical aspect of AI-powered talent matching is its potential to minimize unconscious bias in hiring decisions. Traditional recruitment processes are often plagued by biases—conscious or unconscious—that can skew hiring decisions and undermine diversity and inclusion efforts. AI tools can be programmed to prioritize objective criteria over subjective judgments, focusing on candidates' skills and experiences rather than demographic characteristics. This shift towards data-driven decision-making helps organizations foster a more diverse and equitable workplace.

However, it is essential to acknowledge the challenges and ethical considerations associated with AI in talent matching. While AI tools offer significant benefits, they are not immune to bias. If the data used to train these systems is biased, the algorithms can perpetuate existing inequalities. Therefore, it is crucial for organizations to ensure that their AI systems are transparent and regularly audited for fairness. Implementing robust ethical guidelines and human oversight can help mitigate these risks, ensuring that AI tools contribute positively to recruitment processes.

Incorporating AI into talent matching strategies also requires a cultural shift within organizations. HR leaders and recruiters must embrace data-driven methodologies and be open to adapting their processes to leverage AI's full potential. This transition involves investing in training and development to equip HR professionals with the skills needed to manage and interpret AI systems effectively.

In conclusion, AI tools for talent matching represent a significant advancement in the field of human resources. By enhancing the efficiency, accuracy, and fairness of recruitment processes, these technologies offer a promising solution to the challenges of modern talent acquisition. As organizations continue to explore and implement these tools, they must remain vigilant about ethical considerations and strive to create an inclusive, data-driven recruitment culture.

Challenges in Talent AI

In the rapidly evolving landscape of artificial intelligence, the integration of AI into talent management presents a unique set of challenges. As organizations strive to harness the power of AI to enhance their recruitment and talent development processes, they must confront several key issues to ensure these technologies are used ethically and effectively.

One of the primary challenges in implementing AI in talent management is the potential for bias. AI systems, if not carefully designed and monitored, can perpetuate existing biases present in the data they are trained on. This is particularly concerning in the context of hiring and promotions, where biased algorithms can inadvertently reinforce systemic inequalities. Organizations must therefore prioritize the development of AI systems that are transparent and capable of being audited to ensure fairness. This includes implementing robust mechanisms for regular reviews and updates of AI models to prevent the entrenchment of bias over time.

Transparency is another critical concern. AI systems often operate as 'black boxes,' making decisions without clear explanations of how those decisions are reached. This lack of transparency can lead to mistrust among employees and candidates, who may feel that AI-driven decisions are arbitrary or unjust. To mitigate this, companies must strive to develop AI systems that provide explainable outcomes, where the reasoning behind decisions is accessible and understandable to all stakeholders.

Moreover, the ethical use of AI in talent management involves navigating complex regulatory environments. As governments and regulatory bodies worldwide begin to introduce laws and guidelines governing the use of AI, organizations must ensure compliance with these regulations to avoid legal repercussions. This requires a proactive approach to understanding and integrating regulatory requirements into AI systems from the outset.

The human oversight of AI systems is also paramount. While AI can offer significant efficiencies and insights, it is not infallible. Human oversight is necessary to interpret AI findings accurately and to make nuanced judgments that AI systems may not be capable of. This human-AI collaboration ensures that the technology serves as a tool to augment human decision-making rather than replace it.

Finally, the challenge of maintaining ethical standards in AI-driven talent management cannot be overstated. Organizations must establish clear ethical guidelines and frameworks to guide the development and deployment of AI technologies. This includes fostering a culture of accountability, where the ethical implications of AI use are regularly discussed and addressed by leadership and staff alike.

In summary, while AI holds great promise for transforming talent management, it also poses significant challenges that must be addressed. By focusing on bias prevention, transparency, regulatory compliance, human oversight, and ethical standards, organizations can leverage AI to achieve fairer and more effective talent management outcomes.

Future of AI in Hiring

Artificial Intelligence (AI) is poised to revolutionize hiring practices, offering unprecedented opportunities to enhance efficiency, accuracy, and fairness in recruitment processes. As we navigate the future of AI in hiring, it is crucial to consider both the potential benefits and the challenges that come with its adoption. AI can significantly streamline the hiring process by automating repetitive tasks such as resume screening and candidate outreach. This not only saves time for HR professionals but also allows them to focus on more strategic aspects of talent acquisition. Moreover, AI-driven tools can analyze vast amounts of data to identify the best candidates based on skills and experience, potentially reducing human bias in the initial screening phase.

One of the most promising aspects of AI in hiring is its ability to support skills-based hiring. Traditional hiring practices often emphasize educational background and previous job titles, which can be limiting and exclude talented candidates who may not fit the conventional mold. AI can help shift the focus towards a candidate's skills and competencies, offering a more inclusive approach that recognizes diverse experiences and capabilities. This shift not only broadens the talent pool but also encourages organizations to value potential and adaptability over rigid qualifications.

Additionally, AI can enhance talent attraction by providing personalized candidate experiences. Through AI-powered analytics, organizations can tailor their recruitment marketing strategies to target diverse groups effectively, ensuring that job postings reach the right audience. This personalized approach can improve employer branding and attract a wider range of applicants, fostering a more diverse and inclusive workforce.

AI's potential in assessing culture fit is another area of interest. By analyzing behavioral data and patterns, AI tools can offer insights into how well a candidate might integrate into an organization's culture. However, it is essential to approach this application with caution to avoid reinforcing existing biases.

The key is to ensure that AI systems are transparent, ethical, and regularly audited to prevent discriminatory practices.

Despite these advancements, the integration of AI in hiring is not without challenges. There is a risk that AI systems, if not properly designed and monitored, could perpetuate or even exacerbate existing biases. It is therefore imperative to implement robust ethical guidelines and human oversight in AI-driven hiring processes. Organizations must prioritize transparency and accountability, ensuring that AI tools are used responsibly and that their impact on diversity and inclusion is continuously evaluated.

Looking ahead, the future of AI in hiring holds exciting possibilities for driving meaningful change in workforce diversity and inclusion. By embracing AI's capabilities while addressing its challenges, organizations can move beyond mere diversity rhetoric to implement actionable strategies that foster genuine inclusion. As AI technologies continue to evolve, they offer new frontiers for enhancing workplace inclusion, not just in hiring but throughout the employee lifecycle. The journey towards an equitable workforce is ongoing, and AI can be a powerful ally in achieving this vision.

Moving from Diversity Talk to Action

Understanding Diversity Metrics

Diversity metrics serve as a vital tool for organizations aiming to create inclusive work environments. These metrics provide a quantitative basis for understanding the composition of a workforce in terms of gender, race, ethnicity, age, sexual orientation, disability status, and other dimensions of diversity. By systematically collecting and analyzing this data, organizations can identify disparities, track progress over time, and tailor their diversity, equity, and inclusion (DEI) strategies effectively.

At the core of understanding diversity metrics is the recognition that these metrics are not merely numbers but reflections of an organization's culture and values. They represent the degree to which an organization embraces diversity and inclusion as part of its ethos. When used effectively, diversity metrics can highlight areas where an organization excels in inclusivity and, conversely, where it falls short. This insight is crucial for setting realistic and meaningful DEI goals.

One primary component of diversity metrics is demographic data. This data provides a snapshot of the workforce, showing how diverse it is across various categories. Collecting this data involves asking employees to voluntarily disclose their demographic information, which can include race, gender, age, and other relevant categories. While this process must respect privacy and comply with legal requirements, it is essential for creating a baseline understanding of the workforce's diversity.

Beyond demographic data, diversity metrics also encompass measures of equity and inclusion. Equity metrics assess whether all employees have equal access to opportunities, such as promotions, pay raises, and professional development. Inclusion metrics, on the other hand, gauge the extent to which employees feel valued and integrated into the organizational culture. These might include employee engagement scores, retention rates, and feedback from employee surveys.

The application of diversity metrics extends to various organizational processes. For example, in recruitment, metrics can be used to assess the diversity of candidate pools and the effectiveness of outreach efforts to underrepresented groups. In performance evaluations, they help ensure that assessment criteria are applied consistently across diverse groups, reducing the potential for bias.

However, the effectiveness of diversity metrics hinges on their thoughtful implementation and interpretation. Metrics should be aligned with broader organizational goals and regularly reviewed to ensure they remain relevant. Moreover, organizations must be transparent about their findings and committed to acting on them. This means not only celebrating successes but also addressing shortcomings through targeted initiatives and interventions.

In conclusion, understanding diversity metrics is a critical step towards fostering an inclusive workplace. These metrics provide the data-driven insights necessary to drive meaningful change. By leveraging this information, organizations can move beyond superficial diversity efforts and work towards genuine inclusivity, thereby enhancing their overall performance and reputation. Through continuous assessment and adaptation, diversity metrics can help organizations create environments where every employee feels valued and empowered to contribute their best.

AI's Role in Actionable Insights

Artificial intelligence has emerged as a transformative force in the realm of business intelligence, offering profound capabilities in generating actionable insights. These insights are not merely data points but serve as critical decision-making tools that empower organizations to navigate the complexities of the modern business landscape. AI's ability to process vast amounts of data at unprecedented speeds enables it to identify patterns and trends that would be imperceptible to human analysts. By leveraging machine learning algorithms, businesses can predict future outcomes, optimize operations, and ultimately enhance their strategic planning.

One of the primary advantages of AI in generating actionable insights is its proficiency in real-time data processing. In today's fast-paced business environment, the speed at which information is processed can significantly impact an organization's agility and responsiveness. AI systems are designed to analyze streaming data as it is generated, allowing businesses to make informed decisions promptly. This capability is particularly beneficial in industries where market conditions change rapidly, such as finance and retail, where timely insights can lead to competitive advantages.

Moreover, AI's role in actionable insights extends to its ability to personalize customer experiences. By analyzing customer data, AI can identify preferences and behaviors, enabling businesses to tailor their offerings to meet individual needs. This level of personalization not only enhances customer satisfaction but also fosters brand loyalty. For instance, AI-driven recommendation systems in e-commerce platforms analyze past purchase behavior and browsing history to suggest products that align with the customer's interests, thereby increasing the likelihood of conversion.

AI also plays a crucial role in risk management by providing insights that help organizations anticipate and mitigate potential threats. Through predictive analytics, AI systems can assess risk factors and forecast potential disruptions, allowing businesses to devise contingency plans proactively.

In sectors such as insurance and healthcare, where risk assessment is paramount, AI-driven insights can significantly reduce uncertainties and improve decision-making processes.

Furthermore, AI's capacity for natural language processing enables it to derive insights from unstructured data sources such as social media, emails, and customer reviews. By analyzing sentiment and extracting relevant information, AI can provide businesses with a deeper understanding of customer perceptions and market dynamics. This understanding is invaluable for refining marketing strategies and improving product development.

While the benefits of AI in generating actionable insights are substantial, it is essential to recognize the ethical considerations associated with its use. Ensuring data privacy and avoiding biases in AI algorithms are critical to maintaining trust and integrity in AI-driven insights. Organizations must implement robust governance frameworks to oversee AI applications and ensure compliance with ethical standards.

In conclusion, AI's role in generating actionable insights is a testament to its transformative potential in the business world. By harnessing the power of AI, organizations can unlock new opportunities for growth and innovation, driving success in an increasingly competitive landscape. However, as AI continues to evolve, businesses must remain vigilant in addressing the ethical challenges it presents to fully realize its benefits.

Creating Accountability in DEI

In the pursuit of Diversity, Equity, and Inclusion (DEI), creating accountability is a crucial element that ensures initiatives are not merely performative but lead to tangible outcomes. Accountability in DEI requires a structured approach that aligns with organizational goals and is embedded across all levels of the institution. This involves setting clear expectations, defining measurable objectives, and implementing systems that track progress and impact.

The first step towards accountability is establishing a robust framework that delineates roles and responsibilities. Every stakeholder, from top executives to entry-level employees, must understand their part in fostering an inclusive environment. This clarity of roles not only aids in personal accountability but also in collective responsibility, ensuring that DEI goals are a shared commitment rather than isolated tasks.

Developing key performance indicators (KPIs) specific to DEI is another vital aspect. These metrics should be designed to evaluate both qualitative and quantitative aspects of diversity and inclusion efforts. Quantitative metrics might include the representation of diverse groups within the organization, while qualitative assessments could focus on the inclusivity of workplace culture as perceived by employees. Regular tracking and reporting of these KPIs are essential to create transparency, allowing organizations to adjust strategies as needed and celebrate milestones achieved.

Moreover, accountability is strengthened by embedding DEI into the core values and strategic objectives of the organization. This integration ensures that DEI is not viewed as a separate initiative but as a fundamental aspect of the company's identity and operations.

Leadership plays a pivotal role in this integration, as leaders must champion DEI, model inclusive behaviors, and hold themselves and others accountable for progress.

A culture of feedback and continuous improvement is also critical. Organizations should establish mechanisms for employees to provide input on DEI initiatives, ensuring that their voices are heard and valued. This can be facilitated through regular surveys, focus groups, and open forums. Such feedback loops enable organizations to refine their approaches and address any emerging challenges proactively.

Training and education are indispensable tools in fostering accountability. Providing ongoing DEI training helps equip employees with the knowledge and skills necessary to contribute to an inclusive environment. These programs should be customized to address specific organizational needs and include practical examples that employees can relate to and apply in their day-to-day interactions.

Finally, recognizing and rewarding efforts in advancing DEI can reinforce accountability. By acknowledging individuals and teams who demonstrate commitment to DEI goals, organizations can motivate others to engage actively in these efforts. Recognition can take many forms, from formal awards and public acknowledgment to integrating DEI contributions into performance evaluations and career advancement opportunities.

In essence, creating accountability in DEI is about building a cohesive, transparent, and inclusive framework that permeates every aspect of an organization. It requires a concerted effort from all members of the organization, driven by strategic planning, continuous monitoring, and a steadfast commitment to fostering an equitable workplace.

Case Studies of Successful Implementation

In the realm of human resources and employer branding, the integration of artificial intelligence (AI) has begun to transform traditional practices, offering innovative solutions to age-old challenges. Various organizations have successfully implemented AI-driven strategies to address bias in recruitment processes, enhance career growth opportunities, and foster diverse workplace cultures.

These case studies exemplify the potential of AI to revolutionize HR practices when applied with a focus on ethics and transparency.

One notable example is a multinational corporation that leveraged AI to refine its recruitment process. By utilizing AI-powered language analysis tools, the company was able to identify and eliminate biased wording in job postings, resulting in a more inclusive approach to attracting talent. This initiative not only diversified the applicant pool but also improved the overall quality of candidates, as the language used in job descriptions became more aligned with the company's commitment to diversity and inclusion.

In another instance, a tech company implemented AI solutions to address structural barriers in career progression. By analyzing employee data, AI algorithms identified patterns that suggested disparities in promotion rates among different demographic groups. Armed with these insights, the company restructured its promotion criteria to be more objective and data-driven, ensuring fairer outcomes. This approach not only mitigated bias but also increased employee satisfaction and retention by fostering a more equitable work environment.

Moreover, AI has proven instrumental in measuring and transforming workplace culture. A financial services firm utilized AI-driven sentiment analysis to gauge employee attitudes towards diversity, equity, and inclusion initiatives. The insights gathered helped the organization identify internal resistance and areas needing improvement. As a result, the firm developed personalized AI-driven training programs for leadership, which emphasized inclusive practices and encouraged a culture of openness and respect.

These case studies highlight the importance of ensuring that AI itself is fair, ethical, and transparent. Organizations must conduct regular audits of their AI systems to prevent the reinforcement of existing biases and to maintain trust among stakeholders. Human oversight remains crucial to verify AI decisions and to interpret data within the appropriate context.

The successful implementation of AI in these case studies underscores its potential to drive significant change in HR and employer branding. As AI technology continues to evolve, its role in fostering diversity, equity, and inclusion is expected to expand, offering new opportunities for organizations willing to embrace this transformative tool. However, the journey towards fully realizing this potential requires a steadfast commitment to ethical practices and a willingness to adapt to new challenges and insights brought forth by AI innovations.

Sustaining Long-term Change

To ensure that changes in diversity, equity, and inclusion (DEI) are sustained over the long term, organizations must implement a multifaceted approach that integrates technology, human oversight, and continuous learning. The first step involves leveraging artificial intelligence (AI) to identify and mitigate biases in hiring and promotion processes. AI has the potential to analyze large datasets, revealing patterns of inequality that may not be immediately apparent to human observers. However, this technology must be applied with caution, ensuring that it does not inadvertently reinforce existing biases. This requires regular audits and updates to AI algorithms to maintain fairness and transparency.

In addition to technological solutions, sustaining long-term change necessitates a cultural shift within the organization. This involves fostering an environment where diverse perspectives are valued and integrated into decision-making processes. Leadership plays a critical role in this transformation, as leaders set the tone for organizational culture. Training programs aimed at developing inclusive leadership skills are essential. These programs should focus on equipping leaders with the tools to recognize and address unconscious biases, as well as to create inclusive spaces where all employees feel valued and heard.

Moreover, organizations must establish mechanisms for continuous feedback and improvement. This can be achieved through regular employee surveys and feedback sessions, which provide insights into the effectiveness of DEI initiatives. It is crucial that these feedback mechanisms are designed to be anonymous and accessible, encouraging honest and constructive input from employees at all levels. The data collected should be used to inform ongoing DEI strategies, allowing organizations to adapt and refine their approaches as needed.

Another key element in sustaining long-term change is accountability. Organizations must set clear DEI goals and track progress towards these objectives. This involves not only measuring quantitative outcomes, such as diversity metrics, but also assessing qualitative aspects, such as employee satisfaction and engagement. Transparent reporting of DEI progress is vital, as it holds organizations accountable to their commitments and builds trust with employees and stakeholders.

Finally, partnerships and collaborations can enhance DEI efforts by bringing in external perspectives and expertise. Collaborating with academic institutions, non-profit organizations, and industry groups can provide valuable insights and resources that support DEI initiatives. These partnerships can also help organizations stay informed about best practices and emerging trends in the field of DEI.

In conclusion, sustaining long-term change in DEI requires a holistic approach that combines technology, culture, feedback, accountability, and collaboration. By integrating these elements, organizations can create an environment that not only supports diversity and inclusion but also drives innovation and growth. This ongoing commitment to DEI is essential for organizations looking to thrive in an increasingly diverse and interconnected world.

AI-Driven Inclusion Beyond Hiring

Understanding Inclusion Metrics

In today's rapidly evolving workplace landscape, understanding and implementing inclusion metrics has become a pivotal aspect of ensuring diversity, equity, and inclusion (DEI) within organizations. Inclusion metrics serve as quantitative measures that help managers and leaders assess the effectiveness of their DEI initiatives. These metrics are not just numbers; they are vital tools that provide insights into the inclusivity of an organization's culture, practices, and policies.

At the core, inclusion metrics aim to track the representation and participation of diverse groups within a company. This involves examining the composition of the workforce through various dimensions such as race, gender, age, disability, and more. By analyzing these aspects, organizations can identify gaps and areas where certain groups may be underrepresented or marginalized. This data-driven approach enables companies to set realistic diversity goals and monitor progress over time.

Beyond representation, inclusion metrics delve into the qualitative aspects of the workplace environment. They assess whether employees from diverse backgrounds feel valued, supported, and empowered to contribute fully. Surveys and feedback mechanisms often play a crucial role in gathering this information. Questions might focus on employees' perceptions of inclusivity, experiences of bias or discrimination, and their overall job satisfaction. Analyzing this data helps organizations understand the lived experiences of their employees and identify systemic issues that may hinder inclusivity.

Inclusion metrics also encompass the evaluation of recruitment and retention practices. By examining hiring patterns, organizations can determine whether their recruitment processes are attracting a diverse pool of candidates. Retention metrics, on the other hand, reveal whether diverse employees are staying with the company or leaving prematurely.

High turnover rates among specific demographic groups may indicate underlying issues such as lack of advancement opportunities or an unwelcoming work environment.

Moreover, inclusion metrics are instrumental in assessing the effectiveness of DEI training and initiatives. Organizations invest in various programs aimed at fostering an inclusive culture, such as unconscious bias training, mentorship schemes, and employee resource groups. Metrics help evaluate the impact of these initiatives by measuring changes in employee behavior, attitudes, and perceptions over time. This evaluation is crucial for refining strategies and ensuring that DEI efforts are not just performative but truly transformative.

The integration of technology, particularly AI, has further enhanced the precision and depth of inclusion metrics. AI tools can analyze vast amounts of data to uncover patterns and insights that might be missed by human analysis alone. For instance, AI can identify subtle biases in hiring practices or detect trends in employee sentiment from internal communications. However, it is essential to approach AI with caution, ensuring that these technologies are free from biases themselves and are used ethically.

In conclusion, inclusion metrics are indispensable for any organization committed to fostering a truly inclusive workplace. They provide a clear framework for measuring progress, identifying challenges, and driving meaningful change. By leveraging these metrics, organizations can move beyond superficial diversity efforts and create an environment where all employees feel respected, valued, and able to thrive.

AI in Employee Retention

In the dynamic landscape of modern business, employee retention has emerged as a crucial factor for organizational success. Companies are increasingly turning to artificial intelligence (AI) to address this challenge, leveraging its capabilities to understand, engage, and retain their workforce more effectively. AI offers a multifaceted approach to employee retention, starting with data-driven insights that can transform how organizations understand their employees' needs and motivations.

AI technologies empower HR departments by providing tools to analyze vast amounts of employee data, uncovering patterns and trends that might not be immediately visible through traditional methods. By utilizing predictive analytics, organizations can identify employees who are at risk of leaving and implement targeted interventions to retain them. These analytics consider various factors such as job satisfaction, engagement levels, and even external market conditions, offering a comprehensive view of the workforce dynamics.

Moreover, AI enhances personalization in employee engagement strategies. Through machine learning algorithms, AI systems can tailor communication and development programs to individual employee profiles. This personalized approach ensures that employees receive relevant and timely support, boosting their engagement and satisfaction. For instance, AI can recommend specific training modules that align with an employee's career goals or suggest wellness programs to improve work-life balance, thereby fostering a supportive work environment.

AI also plays a pivotal role in enhancing the feedback loop within organizations. By facilitating real-time feedback mechanisms, AI enables employees to voice their concerns and suggestions through digital platforms. This continuous feedback process not only helps in identifying areas of improvement but also empowers employees by making them feel heard and valued. Furthermore, AI-driven sentiment analysis can assess the emotional tone of feedback, allowing HR teams to address issues proactively and create a positive workplace culture.

In addition to enhancing engagement and feedback, AI supports career development initiatives that are crucial for retention. By analyzing career progression data, AI can identify potential skill gaps and recommend personalized development paths for employees. This proactive approach to career growth not only enhances employee satisfaction but also aligns individual aspirations with organizational goals, reducing turnover rates.

Despite its numerous benefits, the integration of AI in employee retention strategies must be approached with caution. Ethical considerations are paramount, as the misuse of AI can lead to privacy concerns and reinforce existing biases. Organizations must ensure transparency in AI applications, maintaining clear communication about how AI is used and safeguarding employee data.

In summary, AI represents a powerful tool for enhancing

employee retention by providing deep insights, personalizing engagement, and supporting career development. By leveraging AI wisely, organizations can create a more responsive and inclusive workplace, ultimately leading to a more committed and satisfied workforce. As AI technology continues to evolve, its potential to transform employee retention strategies will only grow, making it an indispensable asset for forward-thinking organizations.

Facilitating Inclusive Interactions

In the complex landscape of modern workplaces, fostering environments where every voice is valued is an imperative. Facilitating inclusive interactions is crucial to dismantling barriers and ensuring equitable participation across diverse groups. This process begins with recognizing the subtle biases that often permeate communication, whether in meetings, digital correspondences, or informal interactions. Recognizing these biases requires a conscientious effort to understand and appreciate different cultural backgrounds, communication styles, and personal experiences.

To facilitate inclusivity, organizations must prioritize active listening and empathy. Active listening involves more than just hearing words; it's about understanding the speaker's intent and context. This skill is essential for creating a platform where individuals feel heard and respected. Empathy, on the other hand, enables team members to put themselves in others' shoes, fostering a deeper connection and understanding. These skills can be cultivated through targeted training programs that emphasize the importance of diversity and inclusion in communication.

Moreover, inclusive interactions are supported by the establishment of clear, equitable communication norms. These norms might include guidelines for turn-taking in meetings, ensuring that all participants have the opportunity to contribute. Encouraging open-ended questions and valuing diverse perspectives can also enhance participation from all group members. Leaders play a pivotal role in modeling these behaviors, demonstrating a commitment to inclusion through their own actions and communications.

Technology can also be an ally in this endeavor. AI-driven tools can assist in identifying and mitigating biases in communication. For example, sentiment analysis tools can provide insights into the dynamics of team interactions, highlighting areas where certain voices might be underrepresented or overlooked. By leveraging these tools, organizations can gain a clearer picture of their communication landscape and take proactive steps to address any disparities.

Furthermore, creating a culture of continuous feedback is essential for facilitating inclusive interactions. Feedback mechanisms should be designed to be anonymous and accessible, encouraging honest and constructive input from all employees. Regularly soliciting feedback allows organizations to identify areas for improvement and celebrate successes in their inclusivity efforts.

Ultimately, facilitating inclusive interactions is not a one-time initiative but an ongoing commitment. It requires a deliberate and sustained effort to build an environment where diversity is not only acknowledged but embraced as a strength. By fostering a culture of inclusion, organizations can unlock the full potential of their diverse workforces, driving innovation and success in an increasingly complex and interconnected world.

Case Studies in Inclusion

In the realm of diversity and inclusion, case studies serve as pivotal tools for understanding and implementing effective strategies. Through real-world examples, organizations can glean insights into the practical application of inclusive practices and the tangible benefits they yield. In this exploration, we delve into various scenarios where inclusion has been successfully integrated, highlighting the methodologies, challenges, and outcomes involved.

One notable case involves a technology firm that recognized the lack of diversity within its engineering teams. By conducting a thorough audit of its recruitment processes, the company identified biased language in job descriptions as a significant barrier to attracting diverse candidates. The firm employed AI-powered language analysis tools to revise these descriptions, ensuring they appealed to a broader audience. This proactive approach resulted in a 30% increase in applications from underrepresented groups within a year, demonstrating the power of inclusive language in recruitment.

Another example is a healthcare institution that sought to address disparities in career progression among its staff. The organization utilized AI-driven analytics to examine promotion patterns and identify potential biases in performance evaluations. By implementing a more transparent and data-driven evaluation system, the institution was able to make fairer promotion decisions. This led to a marked improvement in employee morale and a more equitable distribution of leadership positions across gender and ethnic lines.

A third case study focuses on a retail company that faced resistance to its diversity, equity, and inclusion (DEI) initiatives. To tackle this, the company deployed AI-driven sentiment analysis tools to gauge employee attitudes towards DEI efforts. This technology enabled the organization to pinpoint areas of resistance and tailor personalized training programs to address specific concerns. The result was a more supportive workplace culture that embraced diversity as a core value.

Additionally, a financial services firm provides a compelling example of ensuring fairness and transparency in AI applications. Recognizing the potential for AI to perpetuate bias, the firm established rigorous auditing processes for its AI systems. These audits involved both technical evaluations and ethical reviews, ensuring that AI tools adhered to the principles of fairness and transparency. This commitment not only mitigated risks but also built trust among stakeholders, reinforcing the firm's reputation as a leader in ethical AI use.

These case studies illustrate the multifaceted nature of inclusion and the diverse strategies organizations can employ to foster it. From leveraging technology to revising internal processes, the path to inclusion is complex yet rewarding. By learning from these examples, other organizations can craft tailored approaches that align with their unique contexts and objectives, ultimately contributing to a more inclusive and equitable workplace.

Future Directions for AI Inclusion

As artificial intelligence continues to evolve, its role in fostering inclusion within the workplace becomes increasingly pivotal. The future of AI inclusion necessitates a multifaceted approach that not only leverages technology for enhanced diversity but also ensures that AI systems themselves are free from bias. One of the primary areas where AI can make a significant impact is in the hiring process. By utilizing AI-driven tools, organizations can move beyond superficial diversity initiatives to implement actionable strategies that attract and retain diverse talent. These tools can analyze job descriptions, recruitment materials, and employer branding messages to eliminate biased language, thereby creating a more inclusive environment for potential candidates.

Furthermore, the integration of AI in talent acquisition offers the potential for skills-based hiring, which prioritizes a candidate's abilities over traditional metrics such as educational background or previous job titles. This shift not only broadens the talent pool but also allows organizations to identify candidates who might have been overlooked due to non-standard career paths. AI's ability to assess culture fit beyond the hiring stage ensures that diverse talents are not only hired but also thrive within the organization, contributing to a more inclusive workplace culture.

Beyond recruitment, AI plays a crucial role in career development and promotions. Predictive analytics can be employed to identify disparities in career progression, allowing organizations to address structural barriers that may hinder the advancement of underrepresented groups. By providing insights into performance evaluations, AI can help reduce bias and ensure that promotions are awarded based on merit and potential rather than subjective opinions.

As organizations strive to create a more inclusive culture, AI-driven sentiment analysis and feedback mechanisms can help measure and shift workplace attitudes. These tools can detect resistance to diversity, equity, and inclusion (DEI) initiatives and provide personalized training for leadership to foster inclusive practices. Anonymous employee feedback facilitated by AI ensures that all voices are heard and that DEI efforts are continuously improved upon.

However, the deployment of AI in fostering inclusion comes with its own set of challenges. Ensuring that AI systems are fair, ethical, and transparent is paramount. This involves implementing best practices to prevent AI from reinforcing existing biases and conducting regular audits to maintain transparency and accountability. Human oversight remains crucial to monitor AI outcomes and make ethical adjustments when necessary.

Looking forward, the next frontier for AI in workplace inclusion extends beyond hiring and career development. It encompasses creating an environment where AI actively contributes to a culture of belonging and respect for all employees. As AI technologies advance, they offer the potential to revolutionize how organizations approach inclusion, ensuring that diversity is not just a metric but a fundamental aspect of organizational success. By embracing these advancements, organizations can harness AI's full potential to drive meaningful, inclusive change that benefits both employees and the broader community.

The Ethics of AI in HR

Understanding Ethical Challenges

In the realm of human resources and employer branding, the integration of artificial intelligence (AI) presents both opportunities and challenges. Ethical challenges arise primarily from AI's potential to perpetuate biases if not carefully managed. AI systems, when employed in hiring and recruitment processes, can inadvertently reinforce existing inequalities if their underlying algorithms are not scrutinized for bias. This necessitates a comprehensive understanding of the ethical challenges to ensure that AI serves as a tool for fairness rather than discrimination.

One of the primary ethical concerns is the potential for AI to propagate biases present in historical data. AI systems learn from large datasets, which often reflect societal and organizational biases. If these biases are not identified and mitigated, AI can make decisions that disproportionately disadvantage certain groups. For instance, if a dataset used to train an AI system for recruitment primarily consists of data from one demographic, the AI may inadvertently favor candidates from that demographic, thereby excluding others. This challenge underscores the importance of using diverse and representative datasets in AI training.

Moreover, the opacity of AI algorithms poses another ethical challenge. The decision-making processes of AI systems are often described as 'black boxes,' meaning that their internal workings are not easily understood by humans. This lack of transparency can make it difficult to identify when and how an AI system is making biased decisions. To address this, there is a growing demand for explainable AI, where systems are designed to provide clear and understandable insights into their decision-making processes. This transparency is crucial for building trust in AI systems and ensuring accountability.

Another ethical challenge is ensuring that AI systems respect individuals' privacy. AI-driven recruitment tools often analyze vast amounts of personal data to make hiring decisions. It is essential to establish clear guidelines on data usage to protect candidates' privacy and comply with data protection regulations. Organizations must be transparent about what data is collected, how it is used, and who has access to it.

This transparency not only helps in gaining candidates' trust but also ensures adherence to legal and ethical standards.

Additionally, the use of AI in recruitment raises questions about fairness and inclusivity. AI systems must be designed and implemented with a focus on promoting diversity and inclusion. This involves not only eliminating biased language from job postings and employer branding materials but also ensuring that AI systems evaluate candidates based on their skills and potential rather than demographic characteristics. By adopting an inclusive approach, organizations can leverage AI to attract a diverse pool of talent and create a more equitable workplace.

Lastly, there is an ethical imperative to maintain human oversight in AI-driven processes. While AI can assist in making more informed decisions, it should not replace human judgment. Human oversight is essential to interpret AI-driven insights, make nuanced decisions, and address any ethical concerns that arise. This collaborative approach ensures that AI serves as a complement to human expertise rather than a substitute.

In summary, understanding and addressing the ethical challenges of AI in recruitment and employer branding is essential for harnessing its potential while safeguarding against its risks. By focusing on transparency, fairness, privacy, and inclusivity, organizations can use AI as a force for positive change in the workplace.

Frameworks for Ethical AI

In the evolving landscape of artificial intelligence, the integration of ethical considerations into AI frameworks is paramount. As AI systems become increasingly entrenched in decision-making processes, particularly in human resources and employer branding, the potential for bias and inequality looms large. Therefore, establishing robust frameworks for ethical AI is not just a theoretical exercise but a practical necessity to ensure fairness, transparency, and accountability.

Ethical AI frameworks are designed to guide the development, deployment, and governance of AI systems. These frameworks often encompass a set of principles and practices aimed at mitigating biases and promoting inclusivity. One of the core components of such frameworks is the principle of fairness. This principle mandates that AI systems should be designed to treat all individuals equitably, without discrimination based on race, gender, or other personal attributes. To achieve this, AI developers must rigorously test and validate their algorithms against diverse datasets to identify and rectify any potential biases.

Transparency is another critical element of ethical AI frameworks. It involves making the AI systems' decision-making processes understandable and accessible to users and stakeholders. Transparency ensures that individuals affected by AI decisions can comprehend how those decisions were made and challenge them if necessary. This necessitates clear documentation and communication of the AI system's capabilities, limitations, and underlying logic.

Accountability in AI frameworks refers to the responsibility of AI developers and organizations to ensure that their systems operate ethically. This includes implementing oversight mechanisms, such as audits and reviews, to monitor AI systems' performance and adherence to ethical standards.

Organizations must also establish clear protocols for addressing any ethical breaches or unintended consequences arising from AI usage.

Beyond these foundational principles, ethical AI frameworks often include specific guidelines tailored to particular applications. For instance, in HR and employer branding, frameworks may prescribe practices for removing biased language from job postings, ensuring diverse candidate outreach, and using AI-driven insights to support fair promotion and compensation decisions. These guidelines are vital in preventing AI from perpetuating existing inequalities in the workplace.

Moreover, ethical AI frameworks emphasize the importance of regulatory compliance. As governments worldwide develop regulations to govern AI usage, organizations must ensure their AI systems align with legal requirements. This includes adhering to data protection laws, such as the General Data Protection Regulation (GDPR), and staying informed about emerging AI-specific legislation.

The development of ethical AI frameworks is an ongoing process that requires continuous evaluation and adaptation. As AI technology evolves, so too must the frameworks that govern its use. This dynamic nature of ethical AI necessitates collaboration among technologists, ethicists, policymakers, and affected communities to ensure that AI systems serve the broader societal good.

In conclusion, frameworks for ethical AI are indispensable in guiding the responsible use of AI technologies. By embedding fairness, transparency, and accountability into AI systems, these frameworks help mitigate risks and unlock the full potential of AI as a force for positive change.

Balancing Innovation and Ethics

In the rapidly evolving landscape of artificial intelligence (AI), the intersection of innovation and ethics poses significant challenges and opportunities for organizations. As AI technologies become integral to business operations, particularly in human resources and employer branding, the imperative to balance technological advancements with ethical considerations becomes paramount.

This chapter delves into the complexities of fostering innovation while adhering to ethical standards, exploring the dual role AI plays as both a catalyst for progress and a potential perpetuator of bias.

AI's transformative potential in identifying and mitigating bias in recruitment and employer branding is undeniable. By harnessing AI-powered language analysis, organizations can scrutinize job postings and recruitment materials to eliminate biased language, thus creating more inclusive opportunities. This not only broadens the talent pool but also aligns with the growing demand for diversity, equity, and inclusion (DEI) in the workplace. However, the deployment of AI in these areas is not without risks. If not meticulously designed and monitored, AI systems can inadvertently reinforce existing inequalities, highlighting the necessity for a robust ethical framework.

A critical component of this framework is transparency. Organizations must ensure that AI systems are transparent in their operations, enabling stakeholders to understand how decisions are made. This transparency is crucial for fostering trust among employees and applicants, who need assurance that AI-driven processes are fair and unbiased.

Regular audits of AI systems, combined with human oversight, can help maintain this transparency, ensuring that AI tools are not only effective but also ethical.

Moreover, the ethical use of AI extends beyond recruitment to encompass career growth and promotions. AI's ability to analyze career progression data and identify disparities offers a powerful tool for addressing structural barriers. By using predictive analytics, organizations can make more equitable promotion decisions and reduce bias in performance evaluations. However, this requires a commitment to ethical standards and the implementation of safeguards to prevent AI from perpetuating existing biases.

The role of AI in measuring and changing workplace culture is another area where innovation must be balanced with ethics. AI-driven sentiment analysis can uncover internal barriers to DEI initiatives, providing valuable insights into employee perceptions and resistance to change. Personalized AI-driven training programs for inclusive leadership can further support these efforts, fostering a culture that embraces diversity and inclusion. Yet, the ethical implications of using AI to monitor employee sentiment must be carefully considered to protect privacy and maintain trust.

In navigating the path between innovation and ethics, organizations must recognize that the future of AI in hiring and employer branding is not just about technological advancement but about transforming organizational culture. AI offers the potential to move beyond mere diversity talk to real action, driving meaningful change in talent attraction and retention. However, achieving this requires a commitment to ethical practices, ensuring that AI systems are designed and implemented with fairness, accountability, and transparency at their core. By balancing innovation with ethics, organizations can harness the full potential of AI to create workplaces that are not only technologically advanced but also equitable and inclusive.

Role of Policymakers

In the modern landscape of human resources and recruitment, policymakers play a pivotal role in shaping the ethical framework surrounding AI-driven initiatives. As AI technologies become increasingly integrated into hiring and employer branding, the responsibility of policymakers extends to ensuring these technologies do not perpetuate existing biases. Their role is crucial in creating guidelines that promote fair, ethical, and transparent AI practices.

Policymakers must first establish clear regulations that mandate transparency in AI algorithms used for recruitment and career advancement. This involves setting standards for AI audits to ensure that these systems are not only effective but also unbiased. By doing so, they help build trust among organizations and potential employees, who might otherwise be skeptical of AI-driven decisions. Ensuring that AI systems undergo rigorous testing for fairness before implementation is a key area where policymakers can make a significant impact.

Furthermore, policymakers need to advocate for the inclusion of diverse datasets in the development of AI systems. Diverse datasets are crucial in training AI to recognize and mitigate bias effectively. Without this diversity, AI systems are likely to replicate existing societal biases, thus undermining efforts to create equitable workplaces. By enforcing regulations that require diverse data inputs, policymakers can help ensure that AI technologies serve as tools for inclusion rather than exclusion.

In addition to technical guidelines, policymakers should focus on the ethical implications of AI in recruitment. This involves crafting policies that address the moral responsibilities of organizations using AI. Ethical considerations include protecting candidate privacy, ensuring consent for data use, and maintaining transparency about how AI-driven decisions are made. Policymakers can facilitate this by creating frameworks that outline ethical practices and by encouraging organizations to adopt these practices through incentives or penalties.

The role of policymakers also extends to education and awareness. They must work to educate both organizations and the public about the potential and limitations of AI in hiring. This includes dispelling myths about AI capabilities and emphasizing the need for human oversight in AI-driven processes. By promoting a balanced understanding of AI, policymakers can help organizations implement these technologies more responsibly.

Moreover, policymakers have the responsibility to foster collaboration between the public and private sectors to advance AI in a way that benefits all stakeholders. This collaboration can lead to the development of innovative solutions that address the challenges of bias and inequality in recruitment. By facilitating dialogue and partnerships, policymakers can drive the development of AI technologies that align with societal values of fairness and equity.

In summary, policymakers are instrumental in guiding the ethical and fair use of AI in recruitment and employer branding. Through the establishment of transparent regulations, advocacy for diverse data usage, emphasis on ethical considerations, educational initiatives, and fostering collaboration, they can ensure that AI technologies contribute positively to the transformation of modern workplaces. Their efforts are essential in leveraging AI as a force for good, driving real, measurable change in diversity, equity, and inclusion initiatives across industries.

Case Studies in Ethical AI Use

In the realm of artificial intelligence, ethical use is paramount, particularly as AI systems become more integrated into various societal functions. Exploring case studies where AI has been utilized ethically provides valuable insights into best practices and lessons learned. These examples highlight both the potential benefits and challenges of implementing AI in a responsible manner.

One illustrative case involves the use of AI in recruitment processes. Companies have increasingly turned to AI to streamline hiring, aiming to eliminate biases inherent in traditional human decision-making. A notable example is a multinational corporation that implemented an AI-driven tool to analyze job descriptions and candidate profiles. The tool was designed to identify and remove biased language, ensuring a more inclusive recruitment process. This initiative not only broadened the pool of applicants but also demonstrated how AI can be leveraged to promote diversity and inclusion in the workplace.

Similarly, AI has been employed in performance evaluations, providing more objective assessments of employee performance. A tech company adopted an AI system to analyze employee productivity data, reducing the influence of subjective biases from managers. This approach not only enhanced fairness in performance reviews but also encouraged a culture of transparency and accountability. The case underscores the importance of integrating AI with human oversight to ensure ethical standards are maintained.

In another sector, healthcare, AI has been utilized to improve patient outcomes while maintaining ethical considerations. A hospital network implemented AI algorithms to predict patient readmissions, allowing for more targeted interventions. The ethical challenge was ensuring that these predictions did not disproportionately affect certain patient groups. By incorporating ethical guidelines and conducting regular audits, the hospital ensured that the AI system operated transparently and equitably. This example illustrates the necessity of aligning AI applications with ethical frameworks to safeguard against unintended consequences.

The education sector also offers a compelling case study. An educational institution used AI to personalize learning experiences for students. The AI system analyzed student performance data to tailor educational content and identify students who might benefit from additional support. Ethical considerations were paramount, particularly in terms of data privacy and the potential for reinforcing existing educational inequalities. By engaging with stakeholders and implementing robust privacy measures, the institution successfully navigated these challenges, demonstrating the potential of AI to enhance educational outcomes ethically.

These case studies collectively emphasize the importance of a thoughtful approach to AI implementation. They reveal that while AI offers transformative potential, it must be guided by ethical principles to ensure it serves the broader good. Organizations are encouraged to engage in continuous dialogue with stakeholders, conduct regular audits, and remain vigilant about the ethical implications of AI technologies. Through these practices, AI can be harnessed to drive positive change while upholding ethical standards, ultimately contributing to a more equitable and just society.

Transparent AI Systems

Defining Transparency in AI

Transparency in AI is a multifaceted concept that plays a crucial role in the ethical deployment of artificial intelligence technologies. At its core, transparency involves making the functioning and decision-making processes of AI systems understandable to humans. This includes not only the developers and operators of these systems but also the end users and those potentially affected by AI decisions. The importance of transparency in AI cannot be overstated, as it is instrumental in building trust, ensuring accountability, and facilitating the identification and mitigation of biases within AI systems.

One of the primary aspects of AI transparency is the clarity in algorithmic processes. This means that the algorithms used in AI systems should be designed in a way that allows stakeholders to comprehend how inputs are transformed into outputs. This understanding is crucial for debugging, improving system performance, and ensuring that the AI behaves as intended. Transparency in algorithms also involves elucidating the data used for training AI models. This includes providing information on data sources, data collection methods, and any preprocessing steps undertaken before training. Such openness is essential to assess the quality and representativeness of the data, which in turn affects the fairness and accuracy of AI systems.

Another critical dimension of transparency is the interpretability of AI models. Interpretability refers to the degree to which a human can understand the cause of a decision made by an AI system. While some AI models, like decision trees, are inherently interpretable, others, notably deep learning models, are often seen as 'black boxes' due to their complexity. Efforts to enhance interpretability include developing techniques that provide explanations for AI decisions, such as feature importance scores or visualizations of neural network activations. These explanations can help stakeholders understand the rationale behind AI decisions and identify any potential biases or errors.

Transparency also encompasses the communication of AI system limitations and potential risks. This involves clearly stating the conditions under which an AI system is expected to perform well and those under which it may fail. It also includes disclosing any known biases, uncertainties, and assumptions embedded in the system. By being transparent about these aspects, developers can manage user expectations and promote informed decision-making regarding AI deployment.

The implementation of transparency in AI is not without challenges. One of the significant hurdles is balancing the need for transparency with the protection of intellectual property and privacy. Companies may be reluctant to disclose detailed information about their AI systems due to competitive concerns or legal constraints. Additionally, achieving transparency in complex AI models can be technically challenging and resource-intensive. Nonetheless, the pursuit of transparency is vital for fostering ethical AI practices. It requires a collaborative effort from AI developers, policymakers, and researchers to establish guidelines and standards that promote transparency while addressing these challenges.

In conclusion, transparency in AI is a foundational principle that supports the ethical use of AI technologies. By making AI systems more understandable and accountable, transparency helps to build trust and ensure that AI serves the best interests of society. Through continued efforts to enhance transparency, we can unlock the full potential of AI while safeguarding against its risks.

Tools for Transparency

In the realm of artificial intelligence and its application in human resources, transparency is a cornerstone for fostering trust and ensuring ethical practices. AI systems, when used in hiring and employer branding, hold the potential to either mitigate or exacerbate bias. Therefore, implementing tools that enhance transparency is imperative for organizations aiming to leverage AI ethically and effectively.

One of the primary tools for achieving transparency in AI systems is the adoption of transparent algorithms. These algorithms are designed to allow stakeholders to understand the decision-making processes of AI models. By providing insights into how decisions are made—whether in screening resumes or evaluating candidate suitability—organizations can ensure that these processes are free from hidden biases. Transparent algorithms facilitate accountability, allowing HR professionals to justify AI-driven decisions and build trust among employees and applicants.

Moreover, AI audits are crucial for maintaining transparency. Regular audits of AI systems can identify and rectify biases embedded within algorithms, ensuring they function as intended. These audits should be comprehensive, examining data inputs, algorithmic processes, and outputs. By conducting thorough audits, organizations can demonstrate their commitment to ethical AI use, thereby reinforcing their reputation as fair and equitable employers.

Another essential tool is the establishment of human oversight mechanisms. While AI can process vast amounts of data more efficiently than humans, it lacks the nuanced understanding that human judgment provides. By integrating human oversight into AI systems, organizations can enhance decision-making processes, ensuring that AI recommendations are reviewed by HR professionals who can consider context and ethical implications. This hybrid approach balances the efficiency of AI with the empathy and insight of human judgment, promoting fairness and transparency.

Data transparency is also vital for ethical AI use. Organizations must ensure that the data used to train AI models is representative and free from biases. This involves careful data curation and validation processes to prevent skewed or discriminatory outcomes. Transparency in data usage allows stakeholders to understand the origins and limitations of the data, fostering trust in AI-driven processes.

Furthermore, transparent communication with stakeholders is imperative. Organizations should openly share information about how AI tools are used in hiring and employer branding. This includes explaining the purpose and function of AI systems, as well as how they impact decision-making. Transparent communication helps demystify AI for employees and applicants, reducing fears and misconceptions about its role in HR processes.

Lastly, regulatory compliance is a key component of transparency. Adhering to legal and ethical standards ensures that AI systems are used responsibly. Organizations must stay informed about evolving regulations concerning AI use in HR, adjusting their practices accordingly to maintain compliance and protect stakeholder interests.

Incorporating these tools into AI-driven HR practices not

only enhances transparency but also strengthens the ethical foundation of organizations. By prioritizing transparency, companies can harness the benefits of AI while safeguarding against its potential pitfalls, ultimately fostering a more inclusive and equitable workplace.

Challenges in Achieving Transparency

In the quest for transparency within AI-driven systems, organizations face a myriad of challenges that stem from both technical and ethical dimensions. Transparency in AI is critical for fostering trust and ensuring fairness, yet achieving it is fraught with complexities that demand meticulous attention and innovative solutions. One of the foremost challenges is the inherent opacity of AI algorithms. These algorithms, often described as 'black boxes,' operate in a manner that is not easily interpretable. The complexity of machine learning models, particularly deep learning, makes it difficult for even experts to understand how specific inputs are transformed into outputs.

This lack of interpretability poses significant risks, especially when AI is used in high-stakes decision-making processes such as hiring. Without transparency, it becomes nearly impossible to ascertain whether the AI is functioning without bias or fairness. Consequently, there is a pressing need for developing methods that can elucidate the decision-making processes of AI systems. Techniques such as explainable AI (XAI) are being explored to provide insights into how AI models make predictions, thereby allowing stakeholders to understand and trust AI outputs.

Another challenge is the balance between transparency and privacy. While transparency requires that AI systems be open to scrutiny, this must not come at the expense of individual privacy. AI systems often rely on vast amounts of personal data to function effectively. Ensuring that this data is used ethically, and that individuals' privacy is protected, is crucial. Organizations must navigate the delicate balance between providing enough transparency to build trust and maintaining the confidentiality of sensitive information. This requires robust data governance frameworks that define how data is collected, stored, and used.

Moreover, regulatory compliance adds another layer of complexity to achieving transparency. With the advent of regulations such as the General Data Protection Regulation (GDPR) in the European Union, organizations are under increased pressure to ensure that their AI systems comply with legal standards. These regulations mandate that individuals have the right to understand and challenge decisions made by AI, further emphasizing the need for transparent AI systems. Compliance with such regulations not only requires technical adjustments but also necessitates a cultural shift within organizations towards valuing and prioritizing transparency.

Ethical considerations also play a significant role in the quest for transparency. Beyond technical and regulatory challenges, organizations must grapple with the ethical implications of AI transparency. This includes addressing questions about who gets access to information about AI processes and how this information is used. Ensuring that transparency efforts do not inadvertently lead to new forms of bias or discrimination is essential. This requires ongoing dialogue among stakeholders, including technologists, ethicists, and affected communities, to develop ethical guidelines and practices.

In summary, while the path to achieving transparency in AI is riddled with challenges, it is an essential endeavor for fostering trust and ensuring fairness. By addressing the technical, regulatory, and ethical hurdles, organizations can create AI systems that are not only powerful but also transparent and accountable. This requires a concerted effort to advance explainable AI technologies, develop robust data governance frameworks, and engage in meaningful ethical discourse.

Case Studies of Transparent Systems

The exploration of transparent systems within the realm of AI-driven HR practices serves as a compelling illustration of how technology can be harnessed to foster fairness and accountability. Transparency in AI systems is crucial, particularly in human resources, where the implications of bias can profoundly affect career trajectories and organizational culture. Several case studies highlight the transformative potential of transparent AI systems in achieving equitable outcomes.

One notable example involves a multinational corporation that implemented an AI-driven recruitment tool designed to eliminate biases in the hiring process. The system was engineered to evaluate candidates based on a set of predefined competencies, minimizing the influence of subjective judgments. By making the decision-making criteria explicit and accessible, the company ensured that all stakeholders had a clear understanding of how hiring decisions were made. This transparency not only built trust among employees but also enhanced the credibility of the recruitment process.

Another case study focuses on a tech company that faced challenges in promoting diversity within its leadership ranks. To address this, the company adopted an AI-powered analytics platform to scrutinize career progression patterns. The system provided insights into disparities in promotion rates among different demographic groups. By openly sharing these findings with employees and using the data to inform promotion practices, the company was able to make significant strides toward equitable career advancement.

In a different sector, a financial institution utilized AI to conduct sentiment analysis on employee feedback, aiming to identify cultural barriers to diversity, equity, and inclusion (DEI). The transparent nature of the AI system allowed employees to see how their feedback was being interpreted and acted upon. This openness led to a more engaged workforce, as employees felt their voices were genuinely heard and valued.

Furthermore, a retail giant's experience with transparent AI systems underscores the importance of accountability in mitigating algorithmic bias. The company conducted regular audits of its AI tools to ensure compliance with ethical standards. By involving third-party experts in these audits and publicly sharing the results, the company demonstrated a commitment to transparency and ethical AI use. This practice not only enhanced the company's reputation but also set a benchmark for industry standards in ethical AI deployment.

These case studies collectively illustrate the pivotal role of transparency in AI systems. By ensuring that AI processes are open and understandable, organizations can foster trust, improve fairness, and drive meaningful change. Transparent AI systems not only enhance decision-making but also empower organizations to uphold ethical standards, ultimately contributing to a more inclusive and equitable workplace.

Future Trends in Transparent AI

As we look towards the future, transparent AI is expected to play a pivotal role in shaping the landscape of numerous industries, particularly in the realm of human resources and employer branding. The emphasis on transparency in AI systems is driven by the need to build trust and ensure ethical standards are upheld in decision-making processes. One significant trend is the increasing demand for AI systems that are not only transparent but also interpretable. This means that AI models must be designed in such a way that their decision-making processes can be easily understood by humans, allowing stakeholders to gain insights into how conclusions are reached. This is particularly crucial in sectors like HR, where AI-driven decisions can significantly impact people's lives.

Another emerging trend is the development of AI auditing frameworks. These frameworks aim to systematically evaluate AI systems to ensure they adhere to ethical standards, do not perpetuate biases, and maintain transparency. Such audits are expected to become an integral part of AI implementation, providing organizations with the assurance that their AI systems are functioning as intended and without unintended discriminatory effects.

Moreover, there is a growing focus on regulatory measures to govern the use of AI, especially in sensitive areas like hiring and employer branding. Policymakers are increasingly recognizing the need for comprehensive regulations that mandate transparency and fairness in AI applications. This includes requiring companies to disclose how their AI systems operate and the data on which they rely. These regulations are anticipated to evolve continuously, keeping pace with advancements in AI technology.

In parallel, the integration of AI with other emerging technologies is setting the stage for more sophisticated and transparent AI solutions. For instance, the combination of AI with blockchain technology offers promising avenues for enhancing transparency. Blockchain's immutable ledger can provide a verifiable trail of AI decision-making processes, ensuring accountability and traceability.

Furthermore, the rise of explainable AI (XAI) is another key trend that underscores the future of transparent AI. XAI focuses on creating AI systems that can explain their reasoning in human terms, making it easier for users to understand and trust AI-driven decisions. This is particularly relevant in HR, where decisions about hiring, promotions, and compensation need to be transparent to prevent biases and ensure fairness.

Lastly, the role of AI in fostering diversity and inclusion is expected to expand. Transparent AI systems can help organizations move beyond mere compliance towards genuine inclusivity by providing insights into diversity metrics and highlighting areas for improvement. By leveraging transparent AI, companies can develop more inclusive hiring practices and create workplace environments that value diversity.

In summary, the future of transparent AI is poised to be transformative, ushering in an era where fairness, accountability, and ethics are at the forefront of technological advancement. As these trends continue to develop, organizations that prioritize transparency in their AI systems will be better positioned to build trust with their stakeholders and achieve sustainable success.

AI and Regulatory Compliance

Understanding Regulatory Landscapes

Navigating the complex regulatory landscapes surrounding AI in HR is essential for organizations aiming to leverage technology responsibly. The regulatory environment is a critical factor in shaping how AI can be ethically and effectively integrated into hiring and employer branding processes. Regulations exist to ensure that AI technologies do not perpetuate existing biases or create new forms of discrimination. Understanding these regulatory frameworks involves recognizing their intentions and the specific requirements they impose on AI systems.

Regulatory bodies worldwide are increasingly focusing on the ethical use of AI, particularly in areas like employment where decisions can significantly impact individuals' lives. These regulations often mandate transparency, fairness, and accountability in AI systems. For instance, the European Union's General Data Protection Regulation (GDPR) emphasizes data protection and privacy, which are crucial when dealing with AI-driven recruitment platforms that process large volumes of personal information. Similarly, the proposed AI Act in the EU categorizes AI applications based on risk, with employment-related AI tools often falling under high-risk categories requiring stringent compliance measures.

In the United States, the Equal Employment Opportunity Commission (EEOC) plays a pivotal role in enforcing laws against workplace discrimination. As AI tools become more prevalent in recruitment and HR processes, ensuring these tools comply with anti-discrimination laws is paramount. This involves conducting regular audits and assessments to identify and mitigate any biases that AI systems might introduce. Organizations must stay abreast of these regulatory requirements to avoid legal repercussions and maintain ethical standards.

Beyond compliance, understanding regulatory landscapes also involves anticipating future regulatory trends. As AI technology evolves, so too will the regulations governing its use. Organizations need to invest in ongoing education and training to keep their HR teams informed about the latest developments in AI regulation.

This proactive approach not only aids compliance but also positions organizations as leaders in ethical AI deployment.

Moreover, engaging with regulators and participating in industry discussions can provide valuable insights into the regulatory process and help shape future AI policies. By contributing to these dialogues, organizations can advocate for balanced regulations that protect individuals without stifling innovation.

Ultimately, understanding regulatory landscapes is not just about adhering to current laws but also about fostering a culture of ethical responsibility within the organization. This involves embedding ethical considerations into the design and deployment of AI systems and ensuring that all stakeholders are aligned with these values. By doing so, organizations can harness the full potential of AI while safeguarding against its risks, thus driving meaningful and equitable change in their hiring and employer branding practices.

AI Systems and Legal Compliance

Artificial intelligence (AI) systems are increasingly integrated into various sectors, including human resources and employer branding. While these systems offer transformative potential, they also pose significant challenges concerning legal compliance and ethical considerations. The deployment of AI in decision-making processes requires adherence to existing legal frameworks to ensure fairness, transparency, and accountability.

The primary legal concern with AI systems is their propensity to perpetuate or even exacerbate existing biases. Laws and regulations, such as anti-discrimination statutes, are designed to prevent unfair treatment based on characteristics like race, gender, and age. However, AI systems, if not properly overseen, might inadvertently violate these laws by making biased decisions. Therefore, organizations must ensure that their AI tools are designed and implemented in a way that aligns with anti-discrimination laws. This involves regular audits and assessments to detect and rectify any biases in the AI's decision-making process.

Transparency in AI systems is another critical aspect of legal compliance. Many jurisdictions require that individuals have the right to understand how decisions affecting them are made. This transparency is crucial in maintaining trust and ensuring that AI systems operate within the legal boundaries. Organizations must therefore implement mechanisms that allow for the explanation of AI-driven decisions. This could include documentation of the algorithms used and the data sets that inform these algorithms, ensuring that stakeholders can comprehend the logic behind AI decisions.

Moreover, accountability in AI systems is essential to legal compliance. This involves establishing clear lines of responsibility for AI-driven outcomes. Organizations should designate specific roles or committees to oversee AI operations, ensuring that there is accountability for any adverse effects or legal infringements. This accountability is not only a legal requirement but also a best practice to maintain ethical standards in AI utilization.

The evolving nature of AI technology means that legal frameworks must also adapt to address new challenges and opportunities. Policymakers are increasingly focusing on creating comprehensive regulations that encompass the unique aspects of AI systems. These regulations aim to protect individuals' rights while fostering innovation and technological advancement. Organizations need to stay informed about these legal developments to ensure ongoing compliance and to leverage AI technologies responsibly.

In conclusion, the integration of AI systems into organizational processes necessitates a robust approach to legal compliance. This involves not only adhering to current legal standards but also anticipating future regulatory changes. By prioritizing fairness, transparency, and accountability, organizations can harness the full potential of AI technologies while mitigating risks and ensuring compliance with legal and ethical standards.

Risks of Non-Compliance

Non-compliance with ethical standards in AI-driven HR processes can lead to significant risks that organizations must be aware of. These risks are not only legal but also ethical and reputational, impacting the core of an organization's operation and its perception by the public.

One of the primary risks is the potential for reinforcing existing biases rather than eliminating them. AI, when not properly monitored and regulated, can perpetuate the same biases it was designed to eliminate. This occurs when the data fed into AI systems carries historical biases, which the AI then learns and replicates. Consequently, rather than creating a fairer hiring process, AI can inadvertently maintain or even exacerbate inequalities.

Moreover, the lack of compliance with ethical guidelines can result in legal repercussions. Many regions are adopting stringent regulations concerning the use of AI in hiring and employment practices. Non-compliance with these regulations can lead to lawsuits, fines, and other legal actions that can be costly both financially and in terms of an organization's reputation. Companies must ensure they understand and adhere to these regulations to avoid such risks.

Beyond legal and ethical concerns, there is the risk of damaging an organization's reputation. In today's digital age, news of biased AI systems can quickly become public, leading to backlash from both the public and potential employees. This can result in a loss of trust, making it more difficult for organizations to attract and retain top talent. A tarnished reputation can have long-term effects, impacting not just recruitment but also customer loyalty and overall brand perception.

Additionally, non-compliance can hinder internal organizational culture. Employees who perceive their company as unethical or non-compliant with fairness standards may experience decreased morale and engagement. This can lead to higher turnover rates, loss of productivity, and a toxic work environment.

To mitigate these risks, organizations must establish clear, comprehensive compliance frameworks. This involves not only adhering to legal standards but also fostering an ethical culture that prioritizes fairness and transparency. Regular audits and assessments of AI systems should be conducted to ensure they are functioning as intended and not perpetuating biases. Furthermore, there must be a commitment to continuous learning and adaptation as AI technologies and regulations evolve.

Investing in training for HR professionals and other stakeholders on the ethical use of AI can also play a crucial role in compliance. By understanding the potential pitfalls and how to avoid them, organizations can better leverage AI to achieve equitable outcomes. Additionally, engaging with external experts and stakeholders can provide new perspectives and insights, helping to refine and improve compliance strategies.

In summary, non-compliance with ethical standards in AI-driven processes poses significant risks that can affect an organization legally, ethically, reputationally, and culturally. By proactively addressing these risks through robust compliance frameworks and continuous education, organizations can harness the benefits of AI while minimizing potential negative impacts.

Strategies for Ensuring Compliance

In the realm of leveraging artificial intelligence for human resource management, ensuring compliance with ethical standards is paramount. Compliance strategies are crucial to harnessing AI's potential without compromising fairness and transparency. AI systems, while powerful in identifying and mitigating biases, must be employed within a robust framework to prevent reinforcing existing inequalities.

To ensure compliance, it is essential to establish clear guidelines and protocols for AI usage in HR processes. This involves setting up ethical frameworks that define acceptable AI applications and outline procedures for auditing AI-driven decisions. Such frameworks should be developed in collaboration with legal experts, ethicists, and AI specialists to cover all aspects of AI deployment, from data collection to decision-making processes.

A key strategy is the implementation of transparent AI audits. Regular audits are necessary to evaluate the performance and impact of AI systems in HR. These audits should assess whether AI tools are functioning as intended and if they are fair across different demographic groups. By conducting these audits, organizations can identify potential biases and take corrective actions before they cause significant harm.

Human oversight is another critical component of ensuring compliance. AI systems should not operate in isolation; instead, they should be supervised by human operators who can intervene when necessary. This oversight ensures that AI decisions align with the organization's ethical standards and legal requirements. Training programs for HR professionals should include modules on AI ethics and compliance to empower them to effectively oversee AI systems.

Regulatory compliance is also a fundamental aspect of using AI in HR. Organizations must stay informed about the latest legal developments related to AI and ensure their practices align with current regulations. This includes adhering to data protection laws, ensuring data privacy, and obtaining consent from individuals whose data is being used. Compliance with these regulations not only protects the organization from legal liabilities but also builds trust with employees and candidates.

Furthermore, it is essential to foster a culture of continuous learning and improvement within the organization. This involves regularly updating AI systems based on new research findings and technological advancements. By staying abreast of the latest developments in AI ethics and compliance, organizations can refine their strategies to better address emerging challenges.

Finally, engaging with external stakeholders, such as industry bodies and advocacy groups, can provide valuable insights into best practices for AI compliance. These collaborations can offer guidance on navigating complex ethical dilemmas and help develop industry-wide standards for responsible AI use. By participating in these broader conversations, organizations can contribute to shaping the future of AI in HR, ensuring it is used ethically and effectively to drive positive change.

Future Directions in AI Regulation

As artificial intelligence continues to evolve, the regulatory landscape must adapt to address emerging challenges and opportunities. A key focus for future AI regulation will be ensuring that AI systems are developed and deployed in a manner that is ethical, transparent, and fair. This involves creating comprehensive frameworks that address biases inherent in AI algorithms, ensuring that these technologies do not exacerbate existing inequalities.

One of the primary goals of future AI regulation should be to enhance transparency in AI systems. This includes

mandating that AI developers provide clear documentation of how their systems work, the data they use, and
the decision-making processes involved. Transparency is
essential to building trust in AI technologies, as it allows
stakeholders to understand and scrutinize the mechanisms
behind AI decisions. Furthermore, regulatory bodies could
require regular audits of AI systems to ensure compliance
with ethical standards and to identify potential biases.

Another critical area for future regulation is the implementation of ethical guidelines that prioritize human oversight.
While AI systems can process vast amounts of data and
make decisions at unprecedented speeds, human judgment
remains crucial in overseeing these processes. Regulations
should stipulate that AI systems include mechanisms for
human intervention, particularly in high-stakes scenarios
where AI decisions can have significant impacts on individuals or communities.

Data privacy is another significant concern that future AI
regulations must address. As AI systems increasingly rely
on large datasets, often containing sensitive personal information, it is vital to ensure that these systems comply with
data protection laws and respect individuals' privacy rights.
Future regulations could enforce strict data governance

policies, requiring organizations to obtain explicit consent from individuals before using their data and to implement robust data anonymization techniques.

In addition to these foundational principles, future AI regulation should also focus on fostering innovation while safeguarding public interest. This involves striking a balance between encouraging technological advancements and protecting society from potential harms. Regulatory frameworks could include provisions for regulatory sandboxes, where AI developers can test new technologies in a controlled environment, allowing regulators to assess the potential risks and benefits before wider deployment.

Finally, international collaboration will be essential in developing effective AI regulations. As AI technologies transcend national borders, harmonizing regulatory approaches across countries can help prevent regulatory arbitrage and ensure consistent standards globally. International bodies could play a pivotal role in facilitating dialogue between nations, sharing best practices, and developing international guidelines for AI governance.

Overall, the future of AI regulation lies in creating a dynamic and adaptable framework that addresses the ethical, legal, and social implications of AI technologies. By prioritizing transparency, human oversight, data privacy, and international collaboration, regulators can ensure that AI systems are developed and used responsibly, ultimately benefiting society as a whole.

AI and Human Oversight

Importance of Human Oversight

In the rapidly evolving landscape of artificial intelligence, the integration of AI into hiring practices and employer branding presents both opportunities and challenges. While AI has the potential to revolutionize these fields by enhancing efficiency and reducing bias, its deployment must be approached with caution. The role of human oversight becomes paramount in ensuring AI systems do not perpetuate existing biases or introduce new ones. Human oversight serves as a critical checkpoint in the development and implementation of AI-driven processes, particularly in the context of fair hiring and employer branding.

AI systems, when left unchecked, can inadvertently reinforce existing inequalities due to their reliance on historical data that may contain biases. This is where human intervention becomes crucial. By actively monitoring AI systems, humans can identify and rectify biases that the AI might overlook. This oversight is not merely about correcting errors but also about ensuring that AI systems align with ethical and legal standards. It involves a continuous process of evaluation and adjustment to maintain the integrity of AI applications in sensitive areas such as recruitment.

Moreover, human oversight is essential in the interpretation of AI-generated data. While AI can process vast amounts of information and identify patterns, it lacks the nuanced understanding that human judgment provides. Humans can interpret AI outputs within the broader context of organizational goals and values, ensuring that decisions made by AI systems are not only data-driven but also culturally and ethically appropriate. This interpretative role of humans helps in avoiding decisions that, while statistically sound, may be ethically questionable or misaligned with the organization's diversity and inclusion objectives.

The importance of human oversight extends to the transparency and accountability of AI systems. In the hiring process, candidates and employees must have confidence that AI systems are being used fairly and transparently. Human oversight ensures that AI systems are not black boxes whose decisions are inscrutable and unchallengeable. By involving humans in the oversight process, organizations can provide explanations for AI-driven decisions, thereby fostering trust and acceptance among stakeholders.

Furthermore, human oversight plays a vital role in the regulatory and ethical compliance of AI systems. As AI technology advances, regulatory frameworks are evolving to address the unique challenges posed by AI. Human oversight ensures that AI applications adhere to these regulations and ethical guidelines, protecting organizations from legal risks and reputational damage. It involves staying informed about the latest regulatory developments and adapting AI systems accordingly.

In conclusion, while AI offers powerful tools for enhancing hiring practices and employer branding, its integration must be carefully managed. Human oversight is indispensable in this process, providing the necessary checks and balances to prevent bias, ensure transparency, and uphold ethical standards. As organizations continue to leverage AI, the role of human oversight will remain a critical component in achieving equitable and effective AI-driven solutions.

Balancing Automation and Human Input

In the realm of HR and recruitment, the integration of automation with human input is pivotal for creating a balanced approach that leverages the strengths of both. Automation, particularly through AI, offers the ability to process vast amounts of data quickly and identify patterns that might be invisible to the human eye. It can streamline tasks such as resume screening, candidate sourcing, and even initial interview processes, allowing HR professionals to focus on more strategic and interpersonal aspects of hiring.

However, the reliance on automation must be tempered with the understanding that human oversight is crucial. AI systems, while powerful, can inadvertently perpetuate biases present in historical data if not carefully managed. This is where human input becomes essential. HR professionals need to be actively involved in the design and implementation of AI systems to ensure that these tools are used ethically and effectively. They must continuously audit AI outputs to identify and correct biases, ensuring that the technology serves as a tool for inclusion rather than exclusion.

Moreover, the role of human input extends beyond oversight. It involves strategic decision-making that AI cannot replicate. Humans bring empathy, cultural understanding, and ethical considerations that are difficult for machines to emulate. In situations where nuanced judgment is required, such as assessing cultural fit or potential for growth, human insights are invaluable. This highlights the need for a collaborative approach where AI handles the data-driven aspects and humans bring the qualitative assessment to the table.

The challenge lies in finding the right balance. Organizations must develop frameworks that delineate clear roles for automation and human input. This involves setting boundaries for AI's role in the hiring process and ensuring that human judgment is not overshadowed by automated systems. Training HR professionals to understand AI's capabilities and limitations is also crucial. They need to be equipped with the skills to interpret AI outputs and integrate them into their decision-making processes effectively.

Furthermore, transparency in AI processes is vital. Organizations should be open about how AI tools are used in recruitment and what data is being analyzed. This transparency builds trust with candidates and employees, who need reassurance that AI is used fairly and ethically. Regular audits and updates to AI systems can help maintain this trust and ensure compliance with ethical standards.

In conclusion, the integration of automation and human input in HR processes represents a significant evolution in how organizations approach recruitment and talent management. By carefully balancing these elements, companies can harness the efficiency of AI while ensuring that human values and ethical considerations remain at the forefront of their hiring practices. This balanced approach not only enhances the recruitment process but also contributes to building a diverse and inclusive workplace where technology and human insight work hand in hand.

Training for Oversight Roles

In the realm of human resources and employer branding, the integration of Artificial Intelligence (AI) presents both opportunities and challenges. As organizations increasingly adopt AI to enhance efficiency and decision-making, there is a growing need for training individuals to oversee these

AI systems effectively. Oversight roles are crucial in ensuring that AI tools are implemented ethically and do not inadvertently perpetuate biases. This subchapter delves into the necessary training for individuals tasked with these oversight responsibilities, emphasizing the importance of both technical understanding and ethical considerations.

The first aspect of training for oversight roles involves acquiring a comprehensive understanding of AI technologies and their applications in HR. Oversight professionals must be familiar with the mechanics of AI systems, including how algorithms are developed and how they function in analyzing data. This knowledge is essential for identifying potential biases that may arise from algorithmic decision-making. Training programs should therefore include modules on the fundamentals of AI, data science, and machine learning, tailored to the specific applications within HR and recruitment contexts.

Beyond technical skills, training must also focus on ethical issues surrounding AI use. Oversight roles require individuals to be vigilant about the ethical implications of AI-driven decisions. This includes understanding how AI can inadvertently reinforce existing inequalities and being equipped to implement strategies that counteract such biases. Ethical training should cover topics like data privacy, transparency, and accountability. Participants should engage in discussions and case studies that explore the ethical dilemmas encountered in AI applications, fostering a mindset that prioritizes fairness and inclusivity.

Additionally, training for oversight roles should emphasize the importance of continuous monitoring and evaluation of AI systems. Professionals must be adept at conducting AI audits to assess the performance and fairness of these systems regularly. This involves setting up mechanisms for ongoing data analysis and feedback collection from users and stakeholders. By maintaining a proactive approach to monitoring, oversight professionals can swiftly identify and address any issues of bias or discrimination that may emerge over time.

Moreover, effective communication skills are indispensable for those in oversight roles. These individuals must be capable of articulating complex technical and ethical concepts to diverse audiences, including non-technical stakeholders. Training should therefore incorporate components that enhance participants' ability to communicate findings and recommendations clearly and persuasively. This ensures that all stakeholders understand the implications of AI use and are informed about the measures being taken to ensure ethical practices.

In conclusion, training for oversight roles in AI applications within HR is multifaceted, requiring a blend of technical acumen, ethical awareness, and communication prowess. By equipping individuals with these skills, organizations can harness the full potential of AI while safeguarding against the risks of bias and inequality. This comprehensive approach to training not only enhances the effectiveness of AI oversight but also contributes to building a more equitable and inclusive workplace.

Case Studies in Oversight

In the realm of artificial intelligence (AI) and its application in human resources, oversight is a critical aspect that ensures the technology is used ethically and effectively. The integration of AI into HR processes offers the potential to revolutionize recruitment and employer branding. However, without proper oversight, these technologies could inadvertently perpetuate existing biases or create new ones. This subchapter delves into various case studies that highlight the importance of oversight in AI applications within HR, illustrating both the challenges and solutions that have emerged in practice.

One such case involves the use of AI-driven language analysis tools designed to identify and eliminate biased wording in job postings. These tools aim to create more inclusive job descriptions that attract a diverse range of applicants. However, initial implementations revealed that some AI systems reinforced biases due to the data they were trained on. Oversight in this scenario involved regular audits of the AI outputs and adjustments to the training data to ensure fairness and inclusivity. This iterative process underscores the necessity for continuous monitoring and adaptation of AI technologies to align with ethical standards.

Another case study focuses on the use of AI in analyzing career progression and making promotion decisions. AI systems offer predictive analytics capabilities that can highlight disparities in career growth opportunities among different demographic groups. However, the lack of transparency in AI decision-making processes raised concerns about accountability. Oversight mechanisms were implemented, including the establishment of transparent AI audit trails and the involvement of human decision-makers to review AI-generated insights. This hybrid approach not only enhanced the fairness of promotion processes but also built trust in AI systems among employees.

In the context of workplace culture, AI-driven sentiment analysis tools have been employed to detect internal barriers to diversity, equity, and inclusion (DEI) initiatives. These tools analyze employee feedback to identify areas of resistance to change. However, the potential for misinterpretation of data by AI systems necessitated the development of oversight protocols. These protocols included cross-referencing AI findings with qualitative assessments conducted by human DEI experts. By combining AI insights with human expertise, organizations were able to implement more effective strategies for cultural transformation.

The ethical use of AI in HR is further complicated by the need to ensure that AI systems themselves are fair, ethical, and transparent. This includes implementing best practices to prevent AI from reinforcing bias, such as the regular updating of algorithms and datasets. Furthermore, organizations must navigate regulatory and ethical considerations, which require a robust framework for AI oversight. Case studies in this area emphasize the importance of developing clear guidelines and involving multidisciplinary teams in the oversight process to address the complex challenges posed by AI.

Through these case studies, it becomes evident that effective oversight is not a one-time event but an ongoing commitment to ethical AI use. Organizations must remain vigilant in their oversight efforts, continuously adapting to new challenges and advancements in AI technology. By doing so, they can harness the full potential of AI to drive positive change in HR practices, while safeguarding against the risks associated with bias and inequality.

Future of Human-AI Collaboration

As technology continues to evolve at a rapid pace, the collaboration between humans and artificial intelligence (AI) is poised to transform the landscape of various industries. The integration of AI into workplaces offers unprecedented opportunities to enhance productivity, innovation, and decision-making processes. However, this collaboration also necessitates a reevaluation of roles, responsibilities, and ethical considerations to ensure that the benefits of AI are realized without compromising human values.

AI systems are increasingly being designed to complement human capabilities rather than replace them. This synergistic approach allows humans to focus on complex problem-solving and creative tasks while AI handles data processing and analysis at speeds and accuracies unattainable by humans alone. For instance, in the field of healthcare, AI can analyze vast amounts of medical data to identify patterns and predict outcomes, enabling doctors to make more informed decisions about patient care.

In the realm of human resources, AI is being leveraged to streamline recruitment processes, reduce bias, and enhance diversity and inclusion efforts. By analyzing job descriptions and candidate data, AI can help eliminate gendered language and other biases that may deter diverse applicants. Furthermore, AI-driven tools can assist in identifying and promoting talent within organizations by providing data-driven insights into employee performance and potential.

The future of human-AI collaboration also hinges on the development of ethical frameworks and governance structures that prioritize transparency, accountability, and fairness. As AI systems become more autonomous, it is crucial to establish clear guidelines to prevent misuse and ensure that AI-driven decisions align with societal values. This includes implementing robust auditing processes to monitor AI behavior and outcomes, as well as fostering a culture of continuous learning and adaptation among both AI systems and their human counterparts.

Moreover, the rise of AI presents an opportunity to redefine the concept of work itself. As routine tasks become increasingly automated, humans will have more time to engage in activities that require empathy, critical thinking, and emotional intelligence. This shift not only has the potential to enhance job satisfaction but also to drive innovation by encouraging a more diverse range of perspectives and ideas.

However, the transition to a future characterized by human-AI collaboration is not without challenges. It requires a commitment to reskilling and upskilling the workforce to ensure that individuals are equipped with the knowledge and skills needed to thrive in an AI-enhanced environment. Additionally, organizations must actively address concerns related to privacy, data security, and algorithmic bias to build trust and acceptance among employees and stakeholders.

Ultimately, the future of human-AI collaboration is a journey of co-evolution, where both humans and machines learn and grow together. By embracing the strengths of both, society can harness the full potential of AI to create a more equitable, innovative, and prosperous future. This vision requires a collective effort to balance technological advancement with human-centric values, ensuring that AI serves as a tool for empowerment rather than a source of division.

AI's Future Impact on HR

Predictions for AI in HR

The integration of artificial intelligence into human resources heralds a transformative era for both employers and employees. As AI technologies evolve, they are reshaping traditional HR functions, enhancing decision-making processes, and redefining the employee experience. One of the most significant impacts of AI in HR is its potential to mitigate bias in recruitment and promotion practices. By utilizing AI-powered language analysis, HR professionals can identify and eliminate biased wording in job postings and recruitment materials, fostering inclusivity and attracting a more diverse talent pool.

Moreover, AI's capabilities extend to analyzing career progression paths within organizations. By leveraging predictive analytics, AI can unveil disparities in career growth opportunities and promotion decisions, ensuring a more equitable environment. This analytical prowess allows HR departments to make informed, fairer decisions, reducing the influence of unconscious biases that often permeate traditional evaluation methods.

In addition to addressing bias, AI is instrumental in measuring and transforming workplace culture. Through sentiment analysis, AI tools can detect internal resistance to diversity, equity, and inclusion (DEI) initiatives. This insight enables organizations to tailor personalized training programs that promote inclusive leadership, thereby fostering a more supportive workplace environment.

AI also plays a crucial role in collecting and analyzing employee feedback. By facilitating anonymous feedback mechanisms, AI helps organizations gain valuable insights into employee satisfaction and areas for improvement. This feedback loop is essential for driving DEI efforts and ensuring that all voices within the organization are heard and valued.

However, the deployment of AI in HR is not without its challenges. Ensuring that AI systems are fair, ethical, and transparent is paramount. Best practices must be established to prevent AI from perpetuating existing biases. This includes conducting transparent audits of AI systems and maintaining human oversight to guide AI-driven decisions. Additionally, navigating the regulatory and ethical landscape is critical to the responsible implementation of AI technologies in HR.

Looking towards the future, AI holds immense potential to revolutionize hiring and employer branding. It can help organizations transition from merely discussing diversity to taking concrete actions. AI can enhance talent attraction efforts by focusing on skills-based hiring and ensuring cultural fit. Furthermore, the future promises advancements in AI-driven workplace inclusion, extending beyond the realm of hiring to encompass all aspects of employee engagement and development. As organizations continue to adopt AI, the focus must remain on cultivating an ethical framework that balances technological innovation with the principles of fairness and equity.

Long-term Implications for Workforce

As artificial intelligence continues to integrate into the workplace, its implications for the workforce span beyond immediate operational changes. The long-term effects of

AI on employment, skill requirements, and organizational structures are profound and multifaceted. AI technology, while enhancing productivity and efficiency, also presents challenges that organizations must address to ensure a balanced and inclusive future for their employees.

One significant implication of AI in the workforce is the transformation of job roles. As AI systems take over repetitive and data-driven tasks, the nature of work is shifting towards more complex, creative, and strategic functions. This shift necessitates a reevaluation of the skills required by employees, emphasizing the importance of continuous learning and adaptability. Workers need to develop skills that complement AI, such as critical thinking, emotional intelligence, and advanced problem-solving, to remain relevant in the evolving job market.

Moreover, AI's influence on workforce demographics cannot be overlooked. By automating tasks traditionally performed by entry-level positions, AI may reduce the number of such jobs, potentially impacting younger workers and those entering the workforce. This could lead to increased competition for remaining entry-level positions and necessitate enhanced educational and training programs to prepare new entrants for more advanced roles.

Organizations must consider these demographic shifts and invest in reskilling and upskilling programs to support their workforce.

AI also presents opportunities for more inclusive workplaces by mitigating human biases in recruitment and promotions. However, the technology itself must be carefully managed to prevent reinforcing existing biases. Developing fair and transparent AI systems is crucial, as is implementing ethical guidelines and oversight to ensure these systems support diversity and inclusion goals. Organizations must prioritize creating AI tools that enhance fairness in hiring and career progression, allowing for a broader range of talent to thrive.

In addition, AI's impact on organizational structures is significant. As AI systems become integral to decision-making processes, traditional hierarchical structures may evolve into more decentralized models. This can empower employees at all levels to make informed decisions, fostering a culture of innovation and collaboration. However, it also requires a shift in leadership approaches, with leaders needing to be more agile and open to data-driven insights provided by AI technologies.

The long-term implications of AI for the workforce extend to ethical and regulatory considerations. As AI systems become more prevalent, questions about data privacy, autonomy, and accountability arise. Organizations must navigate these challenges by establishing robust governance frameworks that address ethical concerns and comply with regulatory standards. Ensuring transparency in AI operations and maintaining human oversight are essential to building trust among employees and stakeholders.

Overall, the integration of AI into the workforce offers both opportunities and challenges. By embracing AI responsibly and investing in the development of their workforce, organizations can harness the potential of AI to create a more dynamic, inclusive, and innovative work environment. Preparing for these long-term implications requires a proactive approach, focusing on skill development, ethical AI practices, and adaptive organizational strategies.

AI and Global Workforce Trends

The integration of artificial intelligence into the global workforce has been transformative, reshaping industries and the nature of work itself. AI technologies are increasingly being adopted across various sectors, leading to significant shifts in workforce dynamics. This transformation is driven by AI's ability to process vast amounts of data, automate routine tasks, and provide insights that were previously unattainable. As AI continues to evolve, it is essential to understand its impact on the global workforce and the trends that are emerging as a result.

One of the most significant trends is the automation of tasks that were traditionally performed by humans. AI systems are capable of handling repetitive and mundane tasks with higher efficiency and accuracy, freeing up human workers to focus on more complex and creative activities. This shift is not only changing the nature of jobs but also altering the skills that are in demand. As a result, there is a growing need for workers to acquire new skills and adapt to the changing technological landscape. Upskilling and reskilling have become crucial for maintaining employability in an AI-driven world.

Moreover, AI is playing a pivotal role in enhancing decision-making processes within organizations. By analyzing large datasets, AI can identify patterns and trends that might not be immediately apparent to human analysts. This capability enables businesses to make more informed decisions, optimize operations, and improve overall efficiency. Consequently, there is a growing demand for data literacy among the workforce, as employees need to be able to interpret AI-generated insights and integrate them into their decision-making processes.

The geographical distribution of jobs is also being affected by AI. As AI systems enable remote work and collaboration, companies are no longer constrained by geographic boundaries when seeking talent. This trend has led to a more globalized workforce, where individuals from different parts of the world can collaborate on projects without the need for physical relocation. However, this also poses challenges, such as managing a diverse and dispersed team, which requires new approaches to leadership and communication.

Furthermore, ethical considerations are becoming increasingly important as AI technologies are integrated into the workforce. There is a growing recognition of the need to ensure that AI systems are used responsibly and do not perpetuate existing biases or inequalities. Organizations are being called upon to establish ethical guidelines and frameworks to govern the use of AI, promoting fairness and transparency in their operations.

In conclusion, the impact of AI on the global workforce is profound, driving changes in job roles, required skills, and organizational structures. As AI continues to advance, it will be crucial for individuals and organizations to adapt to these changes, ensuring that they can harness the benefits of AI while addressing the challenges it presents. The future of work will be shaped by our ability to integrate AI into the workforce in a way that is both effective and ethical.

Preparing for Future Changes

In the evolving landscape of human resources, the integration of artificial intelligence (AI) represents both a challenge and an opportunity. As organizations strive to harness AI's potential to foster inclusivity and mitigate bias, it becomes essential to prepare for future changes that AI technologies will inevitably bring. This preparation involves understanding the implications of AI, ensuring its ethical application, and anticipating the shifts it will cause in organizational dynamics.

AI's capacity to process vast amounts of data rapidly can help identify biases in hiring practices and employer branding. By analyzing language patterns in job postings, AI can detect and suggest alternatives to biased terminologies, promoting more inclusive communication. This capability is crucial as it encourages the creation of job descriptions that are more appealing to a diverse range of candidates, thus expanding the talent pool. However, for AI to be a genuine ally in this mission, it must be implemented with a clear ethical framework that prioritizes transparency and fairness.

The potential of AI extends beyond recruitment and into the realm of career progression and promotion. Predictive analytics can be leveraged to scrutinize career trajectories and highlight disparities that may exist within an organization. This insight allows for more equitable promotion decisions and helps in reducing bias in performance evaluations. Moreover, AI-driven insights can offer personalized feedback and development plans, catering to the unique needs of employees and fostering an environment of continuous growth and inclusion.

To effectively prepare for the changes AI will bring, organizations must also address the cultural aspects of AI integration. This involves using AI tools for sentiment analysis to gauge employee perceptions and identify resistance to diversity, equity, and inclusion (DEI) initiatives. By understanding these sentiments, organizations can tailor their DEI strategies to address specific concerns and create a more inclusive workplace culture. AI can also facilitate anonymous feedback mechanisms, providing employees with a safe space to express their thoughts and contributing to a more transparent organizational environment.

Ensuring the fairness and transparency of AI systems is paramount. Organizations must establish robust auditing processes to monitor AI applications and mitigate potential biases. This includes maintaining a balance between AI-driven decisions and human oversight to ensure that ethical considerations are not overshadowed by technological capabilities. Regulatory compliance and ethical guidelines should be at the forefront of AI deployment strategies, safeguarding against the reinforcement of existing inequalities.

As AI continues to evolve, its role in hiring and employer branding will expand, requiring organizations to remain agile and forward-thinking. Embracing AI's potential involves shifting from merely discussing diversity to taking tangible actions that leverage AI's capabilities in talent attraction and skills-based hiring. This forward-looking approach will not only enhance recruitment processes but also contribute to building a more inclusive and dynamic workplace. By preparing for these changes, organizations can position themselves as leaders in the ethical application of AI, setting a standard for others to follow in the pursuit of a fairer and more equitable future.

Innovations on the Horizon

As organizations continue to evolve, the integration of artificial intelligence in hiring and employer branding is poised to transform the landscape of talent acquisition and management. AI's capabilities extend beyond current practices, offering a glimpse into a future where technology not only supports but enhances diversity and inclusion efforts within the workplace.

The potential of AI to revolutionize recruitment lies in its ability to minimize human biases, streamline processes, and introduce innovative solutions that were previously unimaginable.

One of the most promising innovations on the horizon is AI-driven talent attraction. By analyzing data from a myriad of sources, AI systems can identify and engage with potential candidates who may not have been considered through traditional recruitment channels. This approach not only broadens the talent pool but also ensures that diverse candidates are given equal consideration. AI tools can assess skills and competencies objectively, allowing for a more inclusive hiring process that values potential over pedigree.

Moreover, AI is set to redefine skills-based hiring, moving away from the conventional reliance on resumes and interviews. By evaluating candidates based on their actual abilities and potential to learn, AI can help organizations identify individuals who might excel in roles despite unconventional backgrounds. This shift towards skills-based hiring emphasizes the importance of adaptability and life-long learning in a rapidly changing job market.

Beyond hiring, AI's role in fostering workplace inclusion is gaining traction. AI can be utilized to monitor workplace interactions and provide insights into the company culture, identifying areas where inclusion efforts may be falling short. By leveraging sentiment analysis and other AI-driven tools, organizations can proactively address issues of exclusion and create a more supportive environment for all employees.

The integration of AI in these domains also raises important questions about ethics and transparency. As AI systems become more embedded in decision-making processes, ensuring that they operate fairly and without bias is crucial. This requires a commitment to transparent AI audits and ongoing human oversight to prevent the reinforcement of existing inequalities.

Looking ahead, the challenge for organizations will be to balance the benefits of AI with the need for ethical considerations. This involves not only implementing AI technologies thoughtfully but also fostering a culture of continuous learning and adaptation. By doing so, businesses can harness the full potential of AI to create more equitable and inclusive workplaces, ultimately driving real, measurable change in their diversity and inclusion efforts.

Call to Action

Recap of Key Insights

In exploring the transformative potential of AI in human resources, 'Beyond the Bias' provides a comprehensive guide for HR leaders, recruiters, and employer branding professionals. The book delves into how AI can be a tool for driving substantial change in recruitment and employment practices, particularly by addressing biases that have long plagued these sectors. As AI technology becomes increasingly prevalent, it offers novel methods for identifying and mitigating bias, yet it also poses the risk of reinforcing existing inequalities if not applied judiciously.

A primary focus is on the role of AI in identifying and eliminating bias in job postings and employer branding. Through AI-powered language analysis, organizations can remove biased wording from job descriptions, creating more inclusive recruitment materials. This technology not only helps in crafting messages that attract a diverse talent pool but also ensures that employer branding aligns with values of diversity and inclusion.

The book further examines structural barriers in career growth and promotions. AI's potential to analyze career progression and highlight disparities is significant. By leveraging predictive analytics, companies can make promotion decisions that are fairer and more equitable, reducing bias in performance evaluations. AI-driven insights thus become pivotal in fostering a more inclusive workplace where career advancement is based on merit rather than unconscious bias.

Changing workplace culture to reduce resistance to diversity, equity, and inclusion (DEI) initiatives is another critical area addressed. AI-driven sentiment analysis tools can detect internal barriers to change, offering personalized, AI-driven training for inclusive leadership. These tools facilitate anonymous employee feedback and DEI reporting, providing organizations with the data needed to measure and transform workplace culture effectively.

Ensuring that AI itself remains fair, ethical, and transparent is emphasized throughout the book. It advocates for best practices that prevent AI from perpetuating bias and stresses the importance of transparent AI audits and human oversight. As organizations navigate the regulatory and ethical landscape of AI in HR, these considerations become crucial for maintaining public trust and achieving genuine progress.

Looking forward, the book envisions a future where AI plays a central role in hiring and employer branding. It outlines the potential of AI to move organizations from merely talking about diversity to taking real action. AI's capabilities in talent attraction, skills-based hiring, and assessing culture fit are highlighted as transformative forces in creating more inclusive workplaces. The journey towards AI-driven workplace inclusion extends beyond hiring, with the promise of fostering environments where all employees have the opportunity to thrive and contribute meaningfully.

Through these insights, 'Beyond the Bias' serves as a roadmap for leveraging AI to create fairer, more equitable hiring practices and workplace cultures. It underscores the necessity of a clear, ethical framework to guide the use of AI, ensuring that its implementation leads to positive, measurable outcomes in diversity and inclusion.

The Path Forward for AI in HR

Artificial Intelligence (AI) is poised to revolutionize the field of Human Resources (HR) by offering innovative solutions to age-old challenges and facilitating more inclusive and efficient processes. As we navigate the evolving landscape of AI in HR, it is crucial to establish a framework that ensures ethical and fair application, maximizing benefits while minimizing potential risks.

One of the primary advantages of AI in HR is its ability to enhance decision-making processes through data-driven insights. By analyzing vast amounts of data, AI can identify patterns and trends that may not be immediately visible to human analysts. This capability is particularly valuable in recruitment and hiring, where AI can help identify the most qualified candidates by evaluating skills, experience, and cultural fit more objectively. Moreover, AI can assist in crafting job descriptions and recruitment materials that are free from biased language, thereby attracting a more diverse pool of applicants.

Despite these advantages, the integration of AI in HR is

not without challenges. A significant concern is the potential for AI systems to perpetuate existing biases if not carefully monitored and calibrated. AI algorithms are trained on historical data, which may contain inherent biases. Therefore, it is essential to implement regular audits and updates to AI systems to ensure they operate fairly and transparently. This includes establishing protocols for human oversight and intervention, particularly in high-stakes decisions such as hiring and promotions.

Additionally, AI has the potential to play a transformative role in employee development and retention. By analyzing data on employee performance and career progression, AI can identify barriers to advancement and suggest targeted interventions. Predictive analytics can inform decisions on promotions and career development opportunities, promoting a more equitable workplace. Furthermore, AI-driven tools can facilitate personalized training programs that enhance skills and foster leadership development, ensuring employees are prepared for future challenges.

AI's role in measuring and influencing workplace culture is another promising area. Through sentiment analysis, AI can assess employee morale and detect areas of resistance to diversity, equity, and inclusion (DEI) initiatives. Such insights can guide organizations in implementing strategies that foster an inclusive and supportive work environment. Moreover, AI can streamline the collection and analysis of anonymous employee feedback, providing a more comprehensive view of organizational culture and identifying areas for improvement.

As AI continues to evolve, its application in HR will likely expand beyond current capabilities. Future developments may include more sophisticated tools for talent management, skills assessment, and cultural integration, all aimed at enhancing organizational performance and employee satisfaction. However, the path forward requires a balanced approach that prioritizes ethical considerations and human oversight, ensuring that AI serves as a tool for empowerment rather than a source of inequity.

In conclusion, the integration of AI in HR presents a compelling opportunity to drive meaningful change and foster a more inclusive and efficient workplace. By leveraging AI responsibly, organizations can enhance their HR practices, attract and retain diverse talent, and ultimately achieve sustainable growth and success.

Encouraging Ethical AI Adoption

In the rapidly advancing field of artificial intelligence, adopting ethical practices is crucial to ensure that technological innovations contribute positively to society. The integration of AI into various sectors, particularly in HR, necessitates a focus on ethical principles to prevent the perpetuation of biases and to promote fairness. Encouraging ethical AI adoption involves several key strategies that organizations and individuals must consider to harness AI's potential responsibly.

One fundamental aspect of ethical AI adoption is transparency. AI systems must be designed and implemented with clear, understandable processes that stakeholders can easily comprehend. This transparency builds trust among users and ensures that the AI's decision-making processes are accountable. Organizations should prioritize open communication about how AI tools work, the data they use, and the outcomes they generate. By doing so, they can mitigate concerns about hidden biases and unfair practices.

Moreover, continuous monitoring and evaluation of AI

systems are essential. This involves regular audits and assessments to ensure that AI tools remain fair and unbiased over time. These evaluations should be conducted by diverse teams to provide varied perspectives and identify potential issues that may be overlooked by homogenous groups. Implementing feedback mechanisms also allows for the identification of unintended consequences and the adjustment of AI systems accordingly.

Ethical AI adoption also requires a commitment to diversity and inclusion. Organizations must strive to create AI systems that reflect the diverse populations they serve. This includes using datasets that are representative and free from historical biases. By incorporating diverse perspectives in the development and deployment of AI, organizations can create more equitable systems that cater to the needs of all users.

Another critical component is the establishment of ethical guidelines and frameworks. These guidelines should outline the principles and values that guide AI usage within an organization. They serve as a benchmark for ethical decision-making and ensure that AI is used in ways that align with the organization's mission and societal values. Training programs and workshops can help employees understand these ethical considerations and apply them in their daily work.

Furthermore, fostering a culture of ethical awareness is vital. Organizations should encourage open discussions about the ethical implications of AI and support initiatives that promote ethical literacy among employees. By creating an environment where ethical considerations are prioritized, organizations can empower their workforce to make informed decisions about AI usage.

Finally, collaboration with external stakeholders, including regulators, academia, and civil society, can enhance ethical AI adoption. These collaborations can provide valuable insights and help shape policies that govern AI usage. Engaging with a broader community ensures that AI systems are designed and implemented with a comprehensive understanding of their societal impact.

In conclusion, encouraging ethical AI adoption is a multifaceted endeavor that requires transparency, continuous evaluation, commitment to diversity, the establishment of ethical frameworks, fostering a culture of awareness, and collaboration with external entities. By focusing on these strategies, organizations can ensure that AI technologies are developed and used in ways that are fair, responsible, and beneficial for all.

Building a Better Future

As we delve into the imperative of building a future that is equitable and inclusive, it is crucial to explore how AI can be harnessed to address and dismantle systemic biases. The integration of AI in HR and recruitment processes presents an unprecedented opportunity to reshape how organizations attract, retain, and promote talent. However, this potential can only be realized if AI technologies are developed and implemented with a commitment to fairness, transparency, and accountability.

AI has the power to transform the recruitment landscape by eliminating bias in job postings and employer branding. By leveraging natural language processing and machine learning algorithms, organizations can identify and remove biased language from job descriptions, ensuring that these materials are inclusive and appealing to a diverse range of candidates. This not only fosters a more diverse applicant pool but also strengthens the organization's employer brand by demonstrating a commitment to diversity and inclusion.

Beyond recruitment, AI can play a pivotal role in addressing structural barriers to career advancement. Predictive analytics can be used to analyze career progression data, identifying patterns of inequity and enabling organizations to make data-driven decisions that promote fairness in promotions and career development. AI-driven insights can help mitigate bias in performance evaluations, ensuring that employees are assessed based on their contributions and potential rather than subjective criteria that may disadvantage underrepresented groups.

Moreover, AI can be instrumental in measuring and transforming workplace culture. Sentiment analysis tools can detect underlying resistance to diversity, equity, and inclusion (DEI) initiatives, allowing organizations to address these issues proactively. Personalized AI-driven training programs can equip leaders with the skills needed to foster inclusive environments, while anonymous feedback mechanisms can provide valuable insights into employee experiences and perceptions of the workplace.

Crucially, the ethical deployment of AI in these contexts requires rigorous oversight and transparency. Organizations must establish best practices to ensure that AI systems do not perpetuate existing biases. This involves conducting regular audits of AI tools, maintaining human oversight in AI decision-making processes, and adhering to regulatory frameworks that safeguard against discrimination. By embedding ethics into AI development and implementation, organizations can build trust with their workforce and stakeholders, ensuring that AI serves as a force for good.

The journey towards a bias-free future is not without challenges. It demands a concerted effort from leaders, technologists, and policymakers to align AI innovations with the broader goals of equity and inclusion. By prioritizing ethical considerations and leveraging AI's capabilities thoughtfully, organizations can pave the way for a future where diversity is not merely a talking point but a fundamental aspect of organizational success. In doing so, they not only enhance their competitive edge but also contribute to a society that values and celebrates diversity in all its forms.

Final Thoughts and Encouragement

As we reflect on the insights shared throughout this book, it becomes evident that the integration of AI into hiring and employer branding is more than just a technological advancement; it is a transformative opportunity. This book has outlined the potential of AI to dismantle biases ingrained in traditional recruitment processes, offering a pathway toward more equitable and inclusive workplaces. However, the journey does not end with understanding these possibilities. Instead, it calls for a commitment to continuous learning and adaptation.

The power of AI lies in its ability to analyze vast amounts of data swiftly and objectively, yet this power must be harnessed with caution and responsibility. Organizations must prioritize the ethical use of AI, ensuring that these tools are designed and implemented to uphold fairness and transparency. This requires a rigorous framework that includes regular audits, human oversight, and adherence to ethical guidelines. Only through such measures can AI serve as a force for good, challenging biases rather than perpetuating them.

Moreover, the responsibility extends beyond the technical aspects of AI. It encompasses a cultural shift within organizations, one that embraces diversity, equity, and inclusion as core values rather than mere aspirations. Leaders and HR professionals must champion this cultural transformation, recognizing that AI is a tool to assist, not replace, human judgment. By fostering an environment where diverse perspectives are valued and encouraged, organizations can unlock the full potential of their workforce.

The future of AI in hiring and employer branding is promising, with opportunities to move beyond surface-level diversity initiatives. AI can facilitate skills-based hiring, enabling companies to identify candidates based on their abilities and potential rather than traditional credentials. Additionally, AI can enhance the alignment between individual values and organizational culture, promoting a more harmonious and productive workplace.

As we look ahead, it is crucial to remain vigilant against the potential pitfalls of AI. This includes being aware of the biases that can be inadvertently encoded into algorithms and the risk of over-reliance on automated systems.

By maintaining a balance between technological innovation and human insight, organizations can navigate these challenges effectively.

Ultimately, the pursuit of fair and inclusive hiring practices is an ongoing endeavor. It requires dedication, introspection, and a willingness to adapt to new insights and technologies. By embracing AI as a partner in this process, organizations can pave the way for a future where talent is recognized and nurtured, free from the constraints of bias. This book serves as a guide and a call to action, encouraging all stakeholders to engage actively in shaping a more equitable world of work.

About the author

Miranda Kingsley's background

Miranda Kingsley is an experienced HR strategist with deep expertise in talent acquisition, employer branding, and diversity, equity, and inclusion (DEI). With a background in HR leadership and consulting, she has supported numerous organizations in designing fair, inclusive, and strategically aligned people processes.

Her career has taken her through various industries, where she has developed innovative recruiting and employer branding strategies. Her focus has always been on bridging technology with human-centered approaches, particularly in leveraging artificial intelligence to enhance talent acquisition and workplace culture. Her expertise includes process optimization, strategic HR management, and using AI to reduce bias in recruitment.

Kingsley firmly believes that technology can revolutionize the HR industry, but only when combined with ethical principles, transparency, and human judgment. Her book „Beyond the Bias" is an analytical yet practical exploration of AI's opportunities and risks in HR. It is based on her extensive experience, academic engagement with economic psychology, and passion for creating a fairer work environment.

Through her work, she aims not only to provide valuable insights for professionals but also to inspire organizations to rethink traditional hiring practices and actively shape the future of work.